# Essential Crochet

# Essential Crochet

Create 30 irresistible projects with a few basic stitches

## ERIKA KNIGHT

Reader's Digest

The Reader's Digest Association, Inc.
Pleasantville, New York/Montreal/
Sydney/Hong Kong

*For all stitch makers passionate for their crafts*

A READER'S DIGEST BOOK
This edition published by The Reader's Digest Association, Inc.,
by arrangement with Quadrille Publishing Ltd

Text and project designs © Erika Knight 2006
Photography, design, and layout © Quadrille Publishing Ltd 2006

FOR QUADRILLE PUBLISHING LTD
Editorial Director: Jane O'Shea
Creative Director: Helen Lewis
Project Editor: Lisa Pendreigh
Pattern Checker: Pauline Turner
Designer: Ros Holder
Editorial Assistant: Laura Herring
Photographer: Graham Atkins Hughes
Stylist: Jane Campsie
Production Director: Vincent Smith
Production Controller: Rebecca Short

FOR READER'S DIGEST
Consulting Editor: Jane Townswick
U.S. Project Editor: Marilyn J. Knowlton
Canadian Project Editor: Pamela Johnson
Project Senior Designer: George McKeon
Cover Designer: Mabel Zorzano
Executive Editor, Trade Publishing: Dolores York
President and Publisher, Books & Music: Harold Clarke

Library of Congress Cataloging-in-Publication Data

Knight, Erika.
  Essential crochet : 30 irresistible projects for you and your home /
  Erika Knight ;
  photographs by Graham Atkins Hughes.
     p. cm.
  ISBN 0-7621-0632-8
     1. Crocheting--Patterns.  I. Title.

TT825.K6213 2006
746.43'4041--dc22

                                    2005050356

Address any comments about *Essential Crochet* to:
The Reader's Digest Association, Inc.
Adult Trade Publishing
Reader's Digest Road
Pleasantville, NY 10570-7000

For more Reader's Digest products and information, visit our website:
www.rd.com (in the United States)
www.readersdigest.ca (in Canada)
www.readersdigest.com.au (in Australia)

Printed in China

1  3  5  7  9  10  8  6  4  2

# Contents

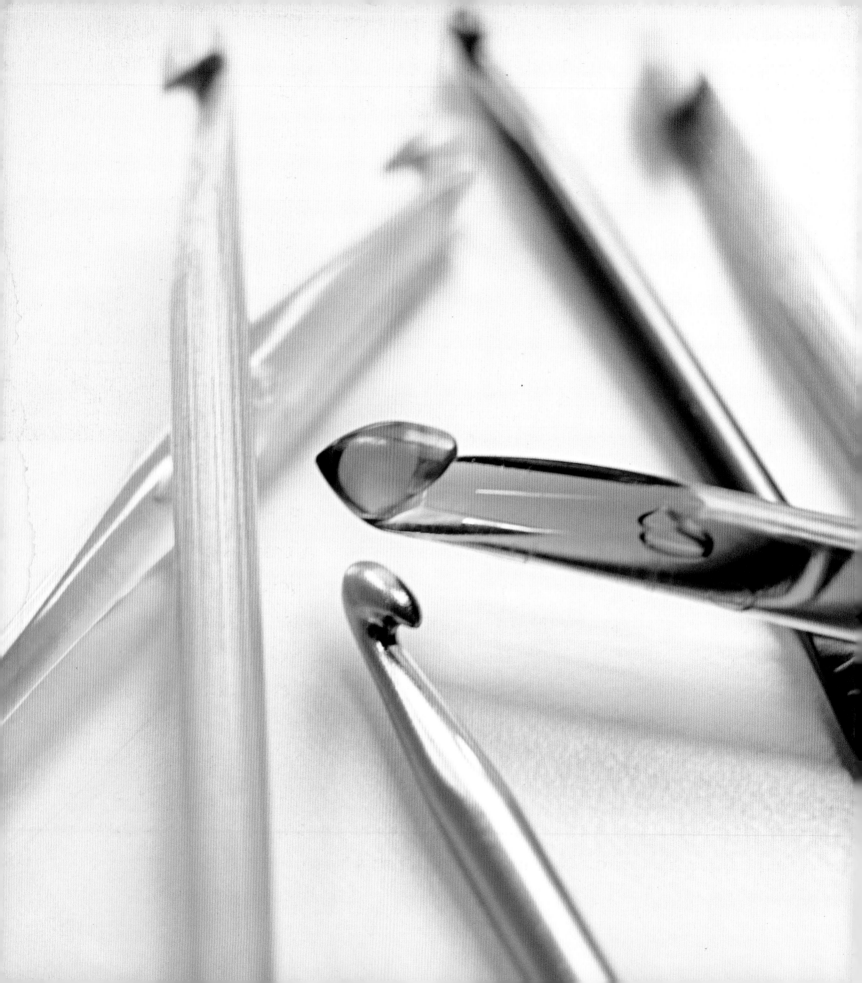

# How to Crochet

There is no simpler form of craft than crochet. Basic yet intricate, delicate yet durable, practical yet decorative, it creates a fabric with an amazingly versatile texture. Crochet is easy because it requires only one hook and a ball of yarn, and you can take it with you anywhere. With only a little practice, you will pick up the techniques quickly and easily and find your fingers working to a rhythm. This book concentrates on a few basic stitches, with which you will be able to make all the projects. I have designed everything in this book to bring crochet up-to-date and make it accessible. But most of all, I want to encourage you to enjoy developing your own creativity as you make the projects in this book.

# Yarns and Texture

You can crochet with a wonderful range of yarns to produce excitingly varied textiles. The yarn and stitches you choose determine the character of the crocheted fabric, which itself is determined by the form and function of the textile. For example, a lap throw requires a strong yarn that will withstand plenty of wear.

You can use the texture of crochet in many ways, often with dramatic results. Some of the projects in this book have been made from unusual materials, such as leather, wire, and string. Some have a tight, dense, and firm structure, while others are more open and flexible.

Crochet can be worked either in rows or in the round, and squares or strips of crochet can be joined together to make patchwork throws. The samples pictured here show the variations in texture and form that can be achieved using a variety of different threads and yarns, ranging from an aran-weight wool and a 4-ply mohair to leather and metallic wire.

# Starting to Crochet

To crochet easily and successfully, you need to hold the yarn and the hook comfortably, with enough tension on the yarn so that when you draw the hook around the yarn, it stays firmly in the indentation of the hook. Most people like to wrap the yarn around their left-hand fingers, and some make an additional wrap around their little finger. Choose whichever yarn-holding method works best for you. Also, hold the hook in whichever way you find most comfortable. Some people prefer a pencil grip, while others hold the hook between the thumb and forefinger of the right hand like a knife. You may even prefer to change your grip, depending on the type of stitch you are working at the time or on the size of the hook.

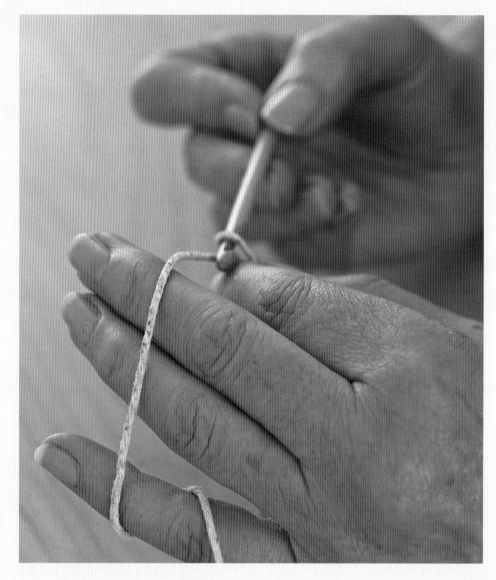

Wrap the ball end of the yarn around the little finger of your left hand, then under the fourth and third fingers, to be held in position between the forefinger and thumb, as shown. When you are starting to crochet, leave a long, loose tail end of yarn on the palm side of your hand so that you can weave this end of the yarn in on the wrong side of the finished project. Hold the hook in your right hand like a pencil.

# Making the First Loop

To start crocheting, you first need to start with a slip knot. There are many different ways you can do this, but the method shown below is very easy to follow.

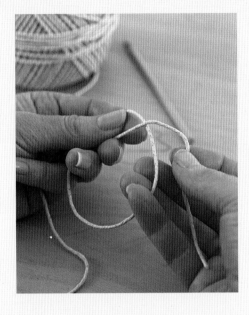

**1** Make a loop in the tail end of the yarn, as shown, crossing the tail end of the yarn over the ball end.

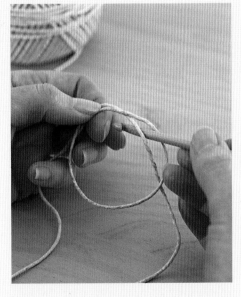

**2** Let the tail end drop down behind the loop; then pass the crochet hook over the loop on the right, catch the tail end with the hook, and pull it through the loop.

**3** Holding the tail end and the ball end of the yarn in your left hand, pull the hook in the opposite direction to create the first loop on the hook. There will be a tight knot under it.

# Making a Foundation Chain

After you have made the slip knot, the next step is to create the foundation chain for the crochet fabric. The project instructions will tell you how many chain stitches to make to start. Chain stitches are also used at the beginning of a row or round and for lace patterns.

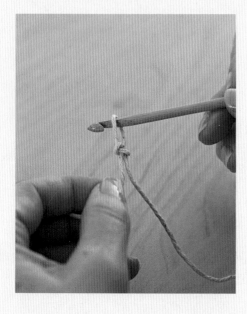

**1** With the slip knot on the hook, grip the tail end of the yarn between the thumb and forefinger of your left hand.

**2** Hold the working yarn taut in your left hand, pass the tip of the hook in front of the yarn, then under and around it. Catch the yarn in the lip of the hook, then draw it through the loop on the hook. This completes the first chain and leaves you with one loop still on the hook.

**3** To make the next chain, pull a new loop through the loop on the hook. Make the number of chains required, keeping the stitches slightly loose, as you will be working into them on your first row.

# Slip Stitch

A slip stitch is the shortest crochet stitch. If you work it into the foundation chain and continue making row after row of it, it forms a very dense, unyielding fabric. It is more commonly used to join the end and beginning of a round, or to work invisibly along the top of other stitches until you reach the required position.

Make a foundation chain (see previous page) of the required length. Insert the tip of the hook through the second chain from the hook. Catch the yarn with the hook (called "wrap the yarn around the hook") and draw it through both the chain and the loop on the hook. This completes the first slip stitch and leaves one loop on the hook. Work the next slip stitch into the next chain in the same way. Continue as required.

# Single Crochet

Single crochet is sometimes also known as "plain stitch." It creates a dense yet flexible fabric, which is ideal for hard-wearing, strong textiles. The easiest of all crochet fabrics to make, it is used frequently in this book in an exciting range of yarns, including soft wool, cotton, and leather. Single crochet and chain stitches can be combined to form other, softer fabrics.

**1** Make a foundation chain the length you require. To make the first single crochet stitch, insert the hook through the second chain from the hook (see slip stitch on previous page). Wrap the yarn around the hook, as shown.

**2** Pull the yarn through the chain, as shown. There are now two loops on the hook.

**3** Wrap the yarn around the hook and pull the yarn through both loops. This completes the stitch.

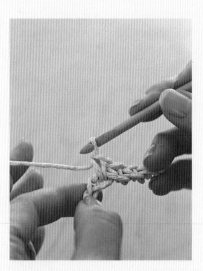

**4** To make the next sc stitch, insert the hook through the next chain, draw a loop through, then draw the yarn through both loops on the hook. Work a single crochet into each of the remaining chains in the same way to complete the first row.

**5** When you reach the end of the first row, finish by inserting the hook through the last two chains when pulling the first loop through, as shown.

**6** To start any subsequent rows of single crochet, turn the work so the loop on the hook is at the right-hand edge. Now make a "turning" chain to take the yarn up to the correct height by drawing a loop through the loop on the hook to form a loose chain, as shown.

**7** Inserting the hook through both loops at the top of the first stitch in the row below, work a single crochet into each single crochet of the previous row. Work following rows in the same way.

# Double Crochet

Double crochet is taller than single crochet. It results in a stitch that is more open and less dense, so it is a flexible, soft textile. It is worked in much the same way as single crochet except that you wrap the yarn around the hook before beginning the stitch. And as it is taller, you begin by working a foundation chain to the required length and then inserting the hook into the fourth chain from the hook.

1  Make a foundation chain to the length you require. Wrap the yarn around the hook, as shown, before inserting the hook into the fourth chain from the hook.

2  Draw the yarn through. There are now three loops on the hook. Wrap the yarn around the hook again, as shown.

3  Draw the yarn through the first, leaving three loops on the hook.

4  Draw the yarn through the first two loops, leaving two loops on the hook, as shown.

5  Wrap the yarn around the hook and draw the yarn through the remaining two loops to complete the stitch, as shown. Wrap the yarn around the hook to begin the next double. Work a double crochet into each of the remaining chains in the same way to complete the row.

6  At the end of the second and subsequent rows, work the last stitch into the top of the three-chain at the edge— wrap the yarn around the hook and pull through the first loop, as shown.

7  Now wrap the yarn around the hook and pull through the first two loops. Wrap the yarn around and pull through the remaining two loops. Work all following rows in the same way. To start any subsequent rows of double crochet, turn the work so the loop on the hook is at the right-hand edge. Make a turning chain of three chain stitches to take the yarn up to the correct height—this counts as the first double crochet in the row. Skip the first stitch in the row below and work the first double into the top of the next stitch.

# Half-double Crochet

The two remaining basic crochet stitches are half-double and treble crochet. A half-double is slightly shorter than a double, while a treble is slightly taller. Try them out following the instructions given below and opposite.

1 Make a foundation chain to the length you require. Wrap the yarn around the hook, as shown, before inserting the hook into the third chain from the hook.

2 There are now three loops on the hook. Wrap the yarn around the hook again.

3 Draw the yarn through all three loops on the hook to complete the half-double crochet stitch. At the beginning of the second row, work two turning chains instead of three.

# Treble Crochet

1  Make a foundation chain to the length you require. Wrap the yarn twice around the hook, as shown, before inserting the hook into the fifth chain from the hook.

2  Draw the yarn through two loops on the hook three times. At the beginning of the second row, work four turning chain instead of three.

# Triple Treble

This makes a very elongated treble stitch. It creates a light and delicate fabric, which is often used in lace patterns.

Make a foundation chain in the length your require. Wrap
yarn around hook three times. Insert hook through work.
Wrap yarn around hook. Draw yarn through (5 loops on hook).
Wrap yarn around hook and draw through first two loops. Repeat
three times until one loop is left on hook. Repeat as required.

# Solomon's Knot

A Solomon's knot is a lengthened chain stitch locked with a single crochet stitch worked into its back loop.

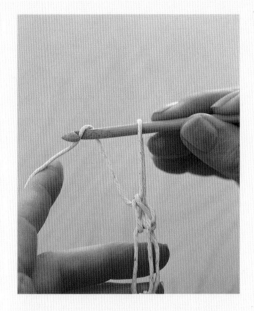

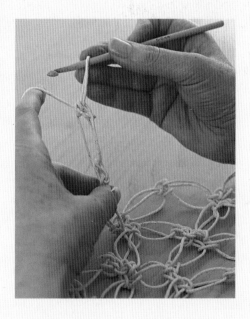

1  Make 1 chain and lengthen the loop as required; wrap the yarn over the hook. Draw through the loop on the hook, keeping the single back thread of this long chain separate from the 2 front threads. Insert the hook under this single back thread and wrap the yarn again. Draw a loop through and wrap again.

2  Draw through both loops on the hook to complete.

3  It is necessary to work back into the "knots" between the lengthened chains in order to make the classic Solomon's knot fabric (see pages 82–5).

# Working in Rounds

Some circular pieces are worked in rounds rather than rows. The stitches may vary, but the basic technique is the same. To begin, make a ring of a few chain stitches as the foundation. The yarn thickness will determine how many chain stitches you make, but generally, for a hole at the center that is drawn closed, about four or six chains will do.

**1** Chain six and insert the hook through the first chain made. Wrap the yarn around the hook in the usual way.

**2** Draw the yarn through the chain and the loop on the hook as for a slip stitch. This forms a foundation ring of chain stitches.

**3** If you are working single crochet into the ring, start by making one chain. (Make three chain if your first round is doubles, two for half-double or four for treble crochet.) Inserting the hook into the ring, work as many stitches into the ring as required to fill the circle.

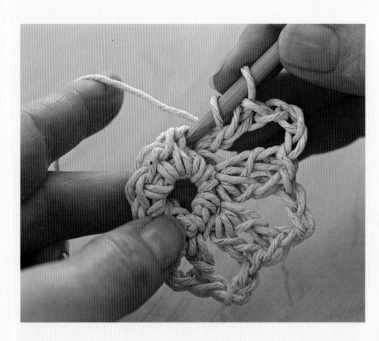

4  To make a motif, continue working in rounds, building up rounds of stitches. Here, a second round of double crochet is being worked into a first round of single crochet.

5  To finish a round, join the round together with a slip stitch to appropriate chain. Continue making rounds, as required.

# Free-form Crochet

A twist on traditional crochet, this is freestyle crochet or couture crochet. Individually designed for you or for your home, free-form crochet is, just as the name suggests, organic, with no fixed pattern or rules. It is endlessly interesting and an innovative approach to traditional crochet.

Basically, free-form crochet is about making an assortment of motifs, and even half motifs, and then linking them together in a random way to create a unique fabric.

Work a collection of various motifs—centers, rosettes, circles—as required. Work small extra groups of treble stitches grafted onto these motifs to make attractive, asymmetrical extensions. (A collection of interesting motifs are given in the patterns for the Molded Wire Mat on pages 86–9, the Organic Table Runner on pages 104–107 and the Free-form Camisole on pages 154–8.) Make some half motifs, if required. (Again, instructions for some of these are given in the pattern for the Free-form Camisole on pages 154–9.)

Simply pin each finished motif haphazardly onto a paper template of your chosen shape. Using a pencil, draw in chain lines between the motifs to link them up as desired, leaving approximately 1½ inches between each motif. While the motifs are still pinned onto the paper template, crochet the linking chains, following the drawn lines, and adding and inserting extra groups of treble stitches at the crossover points of two or more chains. Join the chain to the next motif with a slip stitch and so on.

Analyze your work regularly by eye to create a completely one-of-a-kind and very creative piece of crochet.

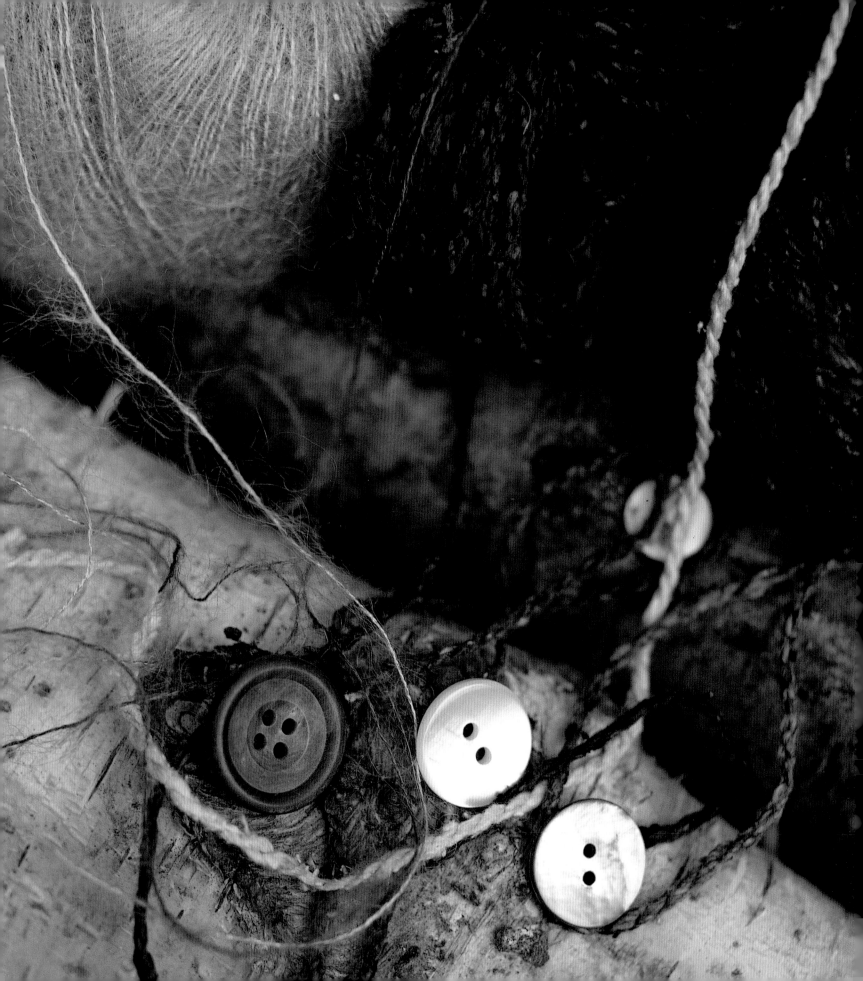

# Basic

This assortment of simple projects, ranging from sumptuous throws and afghans, an elegant wrap, and a cozy scarf, uses the most basic stitches, such as single crochet and double crochet. Worked in textural materials such as tweed, mohair, and leather, these selections reflect the natural elements of the earth. With a warm color palette of fall chestnuts, leaf greens, and lichen, these projects evoke memories of coastal holidays, country days, and family picnics.

# Woven Plaid Afghan

Unashamedly luxurious and extravagant, yet easy to make, this afghan is worked in rich tweeds laced through with velvety chenilles. Its mellow colors are inspired by nature in the fall, but this design would work equally well in bright summer colors. Bands of basic filet crochet have been worked in colorful wool tweeds, which are then woven with threads of chenille that are knotted to form a fringe edging. This design can be interpreted to include as many colors and textures as you like—use up yarns from "end of line" bins or from your own stash—or simply work it in only two or three yarns to complement a particular interior scheme.

# Making the Woven Plaid Afghan

### SIZE
Approx. 74¾ in. (190cm) x 66⅛ in. (168cm)

### MATERIALS
Rowan Yorkshire Tweed Aran or a similar
weight yarn (see page 170) in four colors:
**Color A:** 4 x 3¼ oz. (100g) skeins in brown
**Color B:** 2 x 3¼ oz. (100g) skeins in oatmeal
**Color C:** 4 x 3¼ oz. (100g) skeins in purple
**Color D:** 5 x 3¼ oz. (100g) skeins in green
Rowan Chunky Cotton Chenille or a similar
weight yarn (see page 170) in seven colors:
**Color E:** 1 x 3¼ oz. (100g) ball in taupe
**Color F:** 1 x 3¼ oz. (100g) ball in dark green
**Color G:** 1 x 3¼ oz. (100g) ball in purple
**Color H:** 1 x 3¼ oz. (100g) ball in deep red
**Color J:** 1 x 3¼ oz. (100g) ball in lilac
**Color K:** 1 x 3¼ oz. (100g) ball in light green
**Color L:** 1 x 3¼ oz. (100g) ball in ecru
Hook size J/10

### TECHNIQUES USED
Double crochet and joining in new yarns

For double crochet: see page 16

### GAUGE
This afghan has a gauge of 12dc and 6
rows to 4 in. (10cm) measured over double
crochet using a J/10 hook, or hook size
required to achieve gauge.

### TIP
**Joining in a new yarn:** Begin the last
double crochet in the usual way, but change
to the new yarn when drawing the yarn
through to the last loop of the stitch. Leave
a long, loose end of the old and new yarns
to weave in later or work over the ends for
several stitches before clipping them off.

### METHOD
**Foundation chain:** Using color A, chain 214.
**Foundation row:** Work 1dc into 6th chain
from hook [1 chain, skip 1 chain, 1dc in next
chain] repeat to end. Turn. [105 spaces]
**Row 1:** Chain 4, [1dc into next dc, 1 chain]
repeat to last space, skip 1 chain, 1dc in 4th
of 5th chain. Turn.

#### Stripe pattern repeat
Continuing to repeat row 1 for stitch pattern,
but ending each row with last dc worked
into 3rd of 4 chain, work in stripes as follows:
Color A: 5 rows
Color B: 3 rows

Color C: 5 rows

Color D: 7 rows

Work 20-row stripe-pattern repeat 5 times. Work 5 rows more in color A, so that the afghan ends with 5 rows A to match the beginning edge.

## TO FINISH

Weave any yarn ends into the work. Lay the work out flat. Steam and press lightly.

Cut the chenille yarns into 240½ in. (610cm) lengths. Take three lengths of chenille yarn in your desired color, knot the three lengths together at one end, and use this knot to weave the yarns in and out of the holes made by the crochet.

Once woven into the afghan, knot both ends of the three lengths of chenille yarn, leaving a tassel approx. 4¾ in. (12cm) long at both ends. When all the chenille yarns are woven in the afghan and knotted, trim each tassel to make sure they are all the same length.

# Button-trimmed Scarf

This small scarf, made in basic single crochet, is worked in natural tones of tweed yarns softened with wisps of fine mohair. Crocheted in a random stripe sequence to blend the colors together for a hand-dyed effect, the scarf is trimmed decoratively with mother-of-pearl buttons that reflect the colors of the yarns.

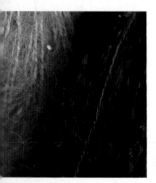  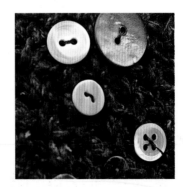

# Making the Button-trimmed Scarf

## SIZE
Approx. 7½ in. x 40 in. (19cm x 102cm)

## MATERIALS
Rowan Summer Tweed or a similar worsted
weight yarn (see page 170) in five colors:
**Color A:** 1 x 1¾ oz. (50g) skein in dark gray
**Color B:** 1 x 1¾ oz. (50g) skein in moss green
**Color C:** 1 x 1¾ oz. (50g) skein in marl gray
**Color D:** 2 x 1¾ oz. (50g) skeins in oatmeal
**Color E:** 1 x 1¾ oz. (50g) skein in lime green
Rowan Kidsilk Haze or a similar light-weight
yarn (see page 172) in two colors:
**Color F:** 1 x 1 oz. (25g) ball in lime green
**Color G:** 1 x 1 oz. (25g) ball in olive green
Hook size G/6
Approx. 40–60 assorted mother-of-pearl or
other decorative buttons

Large sewing needle and dark gray or moss-
green cotton sewing thread

## TECHNIQUES USED
Single crochet and joining in new yarns
For single crochet: see page 14

## GAUGE
This scarf has a gauge of 8½ stitches and 15
rows to 4 in. (10cm) measured over pattern
of 1sc, 1ch, using a G/6 hook, or hook size
required to achieve gauge.

## TIP
**Joining in a new yarn:** Begin the last
single crochet in the usual way, but change
to the new yarn when drawing the yarn
through to the last loop of the stitch.

Leave a long, loose end of the old and new
yarns to weave in later or work over the
ends for several stitches before clipping
them off.

## METHOD
**Foundation row:** Using colors A and G
together, chain 34.
**Row 1:** Using color A, 1sc in 4th chain from
hook [chain 1, skip 1 chain, 1sc in next
chain] repeat to end.
**Row 2:** Chain 2 [1sc in 1st chain space,
chain 1] repeat to end. Turn.
**Stripe pattern repeat**
Continuing to repeat row 2 for stitch
pattern, work in stripes starting with the
third row of color A below the foundation
row (you have already worked the

foundation row in colors A and G and first
2 rows using A above):
* Colors A and G: 1 row
Color A: 9 rows
Color B: 1 row
Color A: 1 row
Color B: 5 rows
Colors B and G: 3 rows
Color C: 1 row
Color B: 1 row
Color C: 2 rows
Color D: 1 row
Color C: 1 row
Color D: 4 rows
Colors E and G: 2 rows
Color E: 6 rows
Color D: 1 row
Color E: 1 row
Color D and F: 1 row **
Color D with random rows of either color F
or G: 81 rows
Repeat the stripe pattern in reverse, starting
from ** and working back to *.

## TO FINISH
Weave any yarn ends into the work.
   Lay the work out flat, then steam and
press lightly.
   Sew the buttons on randomly at both
ends of the scarf using the thread.

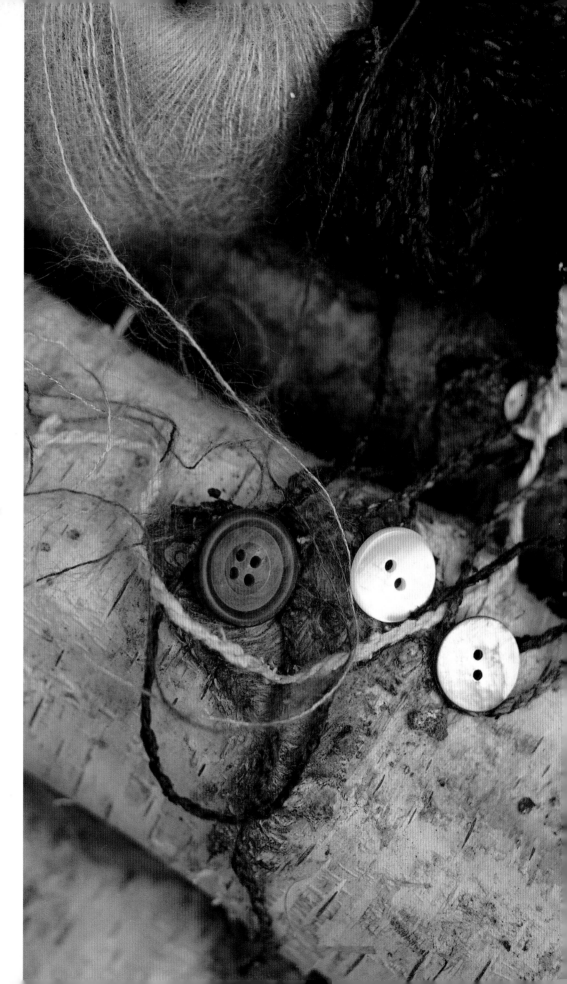

# Textured Round Pillow

The tweed yarn used to make this pillow is combined with silk to create an interesting texture that is very effective. The muted natural hues are all so beautiful that it was hard to choose a single one, so instead I used small amounts of many colors. The pillow is worked in simple rounds of double crochet, using colors in blended bands, then finished with a spiral-stitch trim. This pillow is a very striking accessory for either a modern or traditional décor.

# Making the Textured Round Pillow

**SIZE**
Approx. 18 in. (46cm) diameter

**MATERIALS**
Rowan Summer Tweed or a similar worsted-weight yarn (see page 170) in eight colors:
Color A: 1 x 1¾ oz. (50g) skein in red
Color B: 1 x 1¾ oz. (50g) skein in orange
Color C: 1 x 1¾ oz. (50g) skein in dark brown
Color D: 1 x 1¾ oz. (50g) skein in lime
Color E: 1 x 1¾ oz. (50g) skein in purple
Color F: 1 x 1¾ oz. (50g) skein in red
Color G: 1 x 1¾ oz. (50g) skein in dark red
Color H: 1 x 1¾ oz. (50g) skein in mid brown
Hook size G/6
18 in. (46cm) diameter round pillow form

**TECHNIQUES USED**
Single crochet, double crochet, working in rounds, and joining in new yarns

For single crochet: see page 14

For double crochet: see page 16

For working in rounds: see page 22

**GAUGE**
This pillow has a gauge of 13 stitches and 6 rows to 4 in. (10cm) measured over double crochet using a G/6 hook, but working to an exact gauge is not essential (see Tips).

**TIPS**
**Working in rounds:** When you work in rounds, you never have to turn the fabric. The right side is always facing you.
**Gauge:** Don't worry about gauge too much! Because this pillow cover is made in circles, you can work your stitches in a circle until it is the required size.
**Marking the beginning of a round:** There is no need to mark the beginning of each round because of the color changes.
**Joining in a new yarn:** Begin the last double crochet in the usual way, but change to the new yarn when drawing the yarn through to the last loop of the stitch. Leave a long loose end of the old and new yarns to weave in later or work over the ends for several stitches before clipping them off.

**METHOD**
**Front and Back (make 2)**
**Foundation chain:** Leaving a long, loose end and using color A, chain 4 and join

length of chain into a ring by working a slip stitch into the 1st chain made.

**Round 1 (right side):** Chain 3, work 11dc into ring, working over long, loose end. Join with a slip stitch into 3rd of 1st 3 chain. [12 dc] Change to color B.

**Round 2:** Chain 3, 1dc into same stitch, [2dc into next dc] repeat to end. Join with a slip stitch into 3rd of 1st 3 chain. [24 dc] Change to color C.

**Round 3:** Chain 3, 1dc into same stitch, 1dc into next dc, [2dc into next dc, 1dc into next dc] repeat to end. Join with a slip stitch into 3rd of 1st 3 chain. [36 dc] Change to color D.

**Round 4:** Chain 3, 1dc into same stitch, 1dc into each of next 2dc, [2dc into next dc, 1dc into each of next 2dc] repeat to

end. Join with a slip stitch into 3rd of 1st 3 chain. [48 dc] Change to color E.

**Round 5:** Chain 3, 1dc into same stitch, 1dc into each of next 3dc, [2dc into next dc, 1dc into each of next 3dc] repeat to end. Join with a slip stitch into 3rd of 1st 3 chain. [60 dc] Change to color F. Continue in rounds, increasing 12 stitches on every round by working one more stitch between each increase and changing color each time until round 16 has been worked. Fasten off. The eight-color pattern will have been repeated twice. If necessary, you can add more rounds to achieve the required size.

### TO FINISH

Weave any yarn ends into the wrong side

of the work. Lay the pieces out flat, then steam and press lightly. Join together as follows:

Place the pieces together with the wrong sides facing each other, line up the stitches along the outside edge and pin the layers together around the edges.

Using color A, work a row of sc around the edge until the opening is just large enough to enclose the pillow form. Insert the form and finish the edging by continuing with sc to the end of the round. Join with a slip stitch.

**Next round:** Chain 3, 1sc into each of the 1st 2 chain, then slip stitch into 1st sc, [1sc into next 2sc, 3 chain, 1sc into each of 1st 2 chain, slip stitch in same sc] repeat to end. Fasten off and weave in the end.

# Beaded Cobweb Wrap

Wraps are the perfect accessory, being both practical and stylish. They are easy to wear, can be carried easily, and pack well. Although this wrap is made in whisper-fine silk mohair, it will keep you warm and comfortable. Constructed in a basic open stitch that is quick to make, light, and airy, it is a great project for the beginner, as it grows very quickly. The tiny glass beads are easy to crochet in along the edge for an extra hint of luxury.

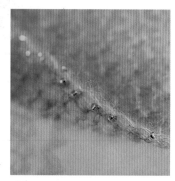

# Making the Beaded Cobweb Wrap

**SIZE**
Approx. 65 in. x 29½ in. (165cm x 75cm)

**MATERIALS**
6 x 1 oz. (25g) balls of Rowan Kidsilk Haze
or a similar lightweight yarn (see page 170)
Hook size J/10
Approx. 250 ⅟₁₆ in. (2.0mm) glass beads
Small tapestry needle

**TECHNIQUES USED**
Single crochet and crocheting in beads
(see pattern)

For single crochet: see page 14

**GAUGE**
This wrap has a gauge of 7½ stitches and
15 rows to 4 in. (10cm) measured over the
pattern using a J/10 hook, or hook size
required to achieve gauge.

**METHOD**
**Foundation chain:** Make 236 chain.
**Row 1:** Work 1sc in 4th chain from hook,
[1 chain, skip 1 chain, 1sc into next chain]
repeat to end.
**Row 2:** 2 chain [counts as 1st sc and 1st
1 chain space] skip 1st sc and work 1sc into
1st 1 chain space, [1 chain, skip next sc,
1sc into next 1 chain space] repeat to end
working last sc into chain space at edge. Turn.
    Repeat row 2 until work measures
29½ in (75cm). Fasten off.

**TO FINISH**
Weave any yarn ends into the work.
Before starting to work, thread half
the beads onto the yarn using a small
tapestry needle.
    Work 1 row of sc, adding a bead on
every stitch, across both short ends of
the wrap.
**Adding a bead in single crochet:** Insert
the hook through the stitch of the previous
row in the usual way, yarn round hook and
draw a loop through. Then slide the bead
close to the work, yarn round hook and
draw through both loops at the same time
pushing the bead firmly on top of the stitch
in the previous row. Weave in the yarn ends
on each short edge.

# Leather Tote Bag

Leather is great to crochet with, although it takes a little time to get used to its particular characteristics. Leather thonging is available in widths from ⅟₃₂–¼ in. (1.0–5.0mm). The maximum size for ease of crochet is probably ⅟₁₆ in. (2.0mm), thicker weights can be more difficult to work with, although they make great bag handles. Make this bag to whatever size suits you, for carrying folders, school books, or shopping. Just knot the bag handles in this simple way, or stitch them securely in position if you will be carrying heavy weights. Experiment with contrasting handles, such as natural or colored braids for a more casual look.

# Making the Leather Tote Bag

## SIZE

Approx. 11½ in. x 10 in. x 4½ in. gusset
(29cm x 25cm x 11.5cm gusset)

## MATERIALS

7 x 55 yd. (50m) balls ¹⁄₁₆ in.- (2.0mm-)
round leather thonging or alternative yarn
(see page 170)
Hook sizes H/8 and J/10
2 x 33½ in. (85cm) lengths ⅛ in.- (5.0mm-)
round leather thonging, for handles

## TECHNIQUES USED

Single crochet

For single crochet: see page 14

## GAUGE

This bag has a gauge of 11sc and 14 rows
to 4 in. (10cm) measured over single

crochet using a J/10 hook, or hook size
required to achieve gauge.

## TIP

**Leather:** Leather is quite hard on the hands,
so when working with it, concentrate on just
one stitch at a time. Warm the leather in
your hands as you work to soften it. It can
become sticky, too, so a little talcum powder
on the hook may assist in pulling it through.

## METHOD

### Front and Back (make 2)

**Foundation chain:** Using J/10 hook, chain 29.
**Row 1:** 1sc in 2nd chain from hook, 1sc in
each chain to end. Turn. [28 stitches]
**Row 2:** 1 chain, 1sc in each sc to end. Turn.
Repeat row 2 until work measures 11½ in.
(29cm). Fasten off.

### Gusset

**Foundation chain:** Using J/10 hook, chain 12.
**Row 1:** As Row 1 given for Front and Back.
[11 stitches]
**Row 2:** As Row 2 given for Front and Back
until work measures 32¾ in. (83cm). Fasten off.

## TO FINISH

Weave any yarn ends into the work.

Attach the gusset to three edges of the
Front by working sc through both layers
using H/8 hook all the way around, working
3sc into the corners, so that the seam is on
the outside. Fasten off. Weave in yarn ends.

Thread a length of thicker leather
through the top edge of the Front of the
bag as shown, then knot securely to make
the bag handles. Repeat for the Back.

# Textured Bed Throw

I love the simplicity of crocheted textures. Just two basic stitches are used to make this sumptuous merino wool throw. Each stitch is used separately to work oversized squares that are alternated to create strips, which are then sewn together to assemble the throw. Although the finished throw is quite heavy because you work only one stitch at a time in crochet, there is no weight to support while making it. This differs from knitting, where the weight of the work is carried on the needles at all times. This lovely bed throw would delight anyone as a beautiful housewarming or wedding gift—make it in classic ecru or add in a contemporary accent color.

# Making the Textured Bed Throw

### SIZE
Approx. 75 in. x 75 in. (190cm x 190cm) to fit a full-size double bed

### MATERIALS
43 x 3¼ oz. (50g) balls Rowan Polar or a similar bulky-weight wool yarn (see page 170)
Hook sizes K/10½ and L/11
Large tapestry needle

### TECHNIQUES USED
Single crochet and half double crochet

For single crochet: see page 14

For half double crochet: see page 18

### GAUGE
This throw has a gauge of 9 stitches and 8 rows to 4 in. (10cm) measured over half double crochet using an L/11 hook, or hook size required to achieve gauge.

### TIP
**Stitch pattern:** When making the bobble squares, take care to check that you have all the bobbles on the same side of the work and that they are all made with the wrong side of the work facing you.

### METHOD
**Foundation chain:** Using L/11 hook, make 37 chain loosely.

**Row 1:** 1sc in 2nd chain from hook, 1sc in each chain to end. [36 stitches] Turn with 1 chain.

**Bobble square**
**Row 2 (wrong side):** 1sc in next stitch, [1tr, 1sc] to last stitch, 1sc, chain 1. Turn.

**Row 3 (right side):** Sc to end, chain 1. Turn.

Repeat these last two rows until work measures 15 in. (38cm).

**Plain square**
Continue working the strip in half double crochet turning each row with 2 chain, for an additional 15 in. (38cm). With right side of the work facing for the next row and starting with row 3, work another 15 in. (38cm) bobble square.

Next, work another 15 in. (38cm) plain square, followed by another 15 in. (38cm) bobble square. Fasten off. You have now completed one strip of five squares.

Make another two strips in the same way that both start and end with bobble squares. Then make two more strips that both start and finish with plain squares.

To start with a 15 in. (38cm) plain square, make 38 chain and work 1 half double in 3rd chain from hook, then half double to end. [36 stitches]

## TO FINISH

Weave any yarn ends into the work. Join alternating strips together with small, neat whip stitches using the tapestry needle.

Using hook size K/10½, work 3 rows of sc all round the edge, working 3sc into each corner, 1sc into each stitch along top and bottom and 1sc into each row along sides. Make sure that the work is not puckering up as you go. Fasten off.

Weave in any remaining yarn ends.

# Timeless

These quintessentially elegant and collectible pieces hark back to the traditions of crochet while simplifying and updating them for today. Motifs worked in the round are synonymous with the craft of crochet, so here I have created a classic patchwork throw, using this simple shape. Crochet also lends itself superbly to fine lace and filet work, so included in this section is a selection of my favorite pieces, from lace edgings for pillowcases and bed linens to filet-work pillows, that are sheer perfection.

# String Ottoman

Natural string has a great matte finish, an interesting texture and stitch clarity, and it is great for projects around the home. Although it requires a little more patience to work with, as it is not a conventional yarn, the results are striking. This simple ottoman is made from a round-motif top and bottom, with an easy cluster stitch section in the middle. Seek out old ottomans from thrift stores to recover or use precut foam from fabric stores.

# Making the String Ottoman

## SIZE
Approx. 11 in. (18cm) high x 15 in. (38cm) diameter, but measurements can be easily adjusted as required; purchase a commercial ottoman or cut foam to size.

## MATERIALS
9 x 98 yd. (89m) balls thick kitchen twine (from a hardware store, see page 170)
Hook size F/5 or hook size required to achieve gauge
Tapestry needle
Fabric to cover ottoman (optional)

## TECHNIQUES USED
Single crochet and treble crochet, and working in rounds

For single crochet: see page 14

For treble crochet: see page 19

For working in rounds: see page 22

## GAUGE
This ottoman has a gauge of 6½ clusters and 7 rows to 4 in. (10cm) measured over cluster pattern rows using an F/5 hook, but working to an exact gauge is not essential (see Tips).

## TIPS
**Working in rounds:** When you work in rounds, you never have to turn the fabric. The right side is always facing you.

**Gauge:** Don't worry about gauge too much! Because this stool cover is made in circles, you can work your stitches in rounds until it is the required size.

**Marking the beginning of a round:** Mark the beginning of each round to make it easier to keep your place.

## METHOD
**Top and center (worked as one piece)**
**Foundation chain:** Leaving a long, loose tail of yarn, chain 8 and join length of chain into ring by working a slip stitch into 1st chain made.
**Round 1:** Chain 2 to count as 1st sc, work 15sc into circle. Join with a slip stitch into 2nd of 1st 2 chain. [16 stitches]
**Round 2:** Chain 4 to count as 1st tr, 1tr

**Round 10:** Chain 3, * 1 cluster (yarn around hook, insert hook between next 2 trebles, draw through a loop, yarn round hook, draw through 2 loops) 3 times in the same space, yarn round hook, draw through 4 loops, chain 1, skip next space, repeat from * to end, omitting last 1 chain of repeat. Join with a slip stitch into 3rd of 3 chain. [80 clusters]

**Round 11:** Chain 3, * 1 cluster in chain between clusters of previous row, chain 1, repeat from * to end and join with a slip stitch into 3rd of 3 chain.

Repeat Round 11 until work measures approx. 9½ in. (24cm) or required length. Adjust the length here to fit the height of your ottoman, less 1 in. (2.5cm) to allow cover to fit tightly. Fasten off. Weave in any yarn ends.

### Base

Work Rounds 1 to 9 as given for Top. Fasten off. Weave in any yarn ends.

### TO FINISH

If necessary, cover a foam ottoman with fabric. Cut two fabric circles to the size of the top and base, adding a ¾-in. (1.5-cm) seam allowance all the way around, and cut a fabric strip to the size of the middle section, adding a ¾-in. (1.5-cm) seam allowance around all edges. Sew the middle section to the top circle. Sew the middle section seam. Turn right side out and slip the sewn cover over the foam inner. Sew the bottom circle to the middle section to enclose, using small, neat whip stitches. Slip the crocheted top and middle section over and again slip stitch the crochet bottom to finish. Sew in final yarn ends to the wrong side of the work.

into next sc, * chain 4, 2tr, repeat from * to end, chain 4. Join with a slip stitch into 4th of 1st 4 chain.

**Round 3:** Slip stitch into next tr and into 1st 4 chain space, chain 4, 5tr into same space, * chain 3, 6tr into next space, repeat from * to end, chain 3. Join with a slip stitch into 4th of 1st 4 chain.

**Round 4:** Chain 4, 1tr into same place as last slip stitch, * 4tr, 2tr into next tr, 4 chain, 2tr into next tr, repeat from * to end, omitting 2tr at end of last repeat. Join with a slip stitch into 4th of 1st 4 chain.

**Round 5:** Chain 4, 7tr leaving last loop of each tr on hook, yarn round hook and draw through all loops on hook, * chain 8, 1sc into next space, chain 8, 8tr leaving last loop of each tr on hook, yarn round hook and draw through all loops on hook—called treble cluster—repeat from *

ending with 8 chain, 1sc into next space, 8 chain. Join with a slip stitch into top of 1st treble cluster.

**Round 6:** Slip stitch into each of next 4 chain, 1sc into loop, * chain 9, 1sc into next loop, repeat from * ending with 9 chain. Join with a slip stitch into 1st sc.

**Round 7:** Slip stitch into each of next 3 chain, chain 4, 4tr into same loop, * chain 5, 5tr into next loop, repeat from * ending with 5 chain. Join with a slip stitch into 4th of 1st chain.

**Round 8:** 1sc into same place as last slip stitch, 1sc into each of next 4tr, * 5sc into next space, 1sc into each of next 5tr, repeat from * ending with 5sc into last space. Join with a slip stitch into 1st sc.

**Round 9:** Chain 4, 1tr into every sc to end. Join with a slip stitch into top of chain. [160 trebles]

# Satin Lingerie Case

This luxurious lingerie case is crocheted in a cluster stitch that creates a firm fabric with an attractive texture that gives a vintage feel. It is made very simply in a long strip, which is then folded and stitched. The natural finish of the scallop stitch gives a lovely edge detail. The bag is lined in satin for pure indulgence, and a big attached chocolate-colored bow is an added touch of luxury. Make a larger bag for pajamas and a smaller one for jewelry or other favorite accessories.

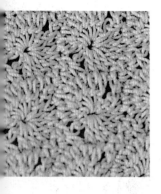
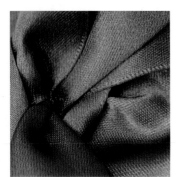

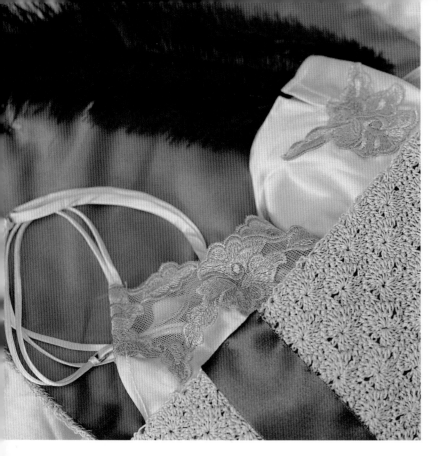

# Making the Satin Lingerie Case

## SIZE
Approx. 8 in. x 10½ in. (20cm x 27cm)

## MATERIALS
3 x 1¾ oz. (50g) balls Coats Aida or similar no. 5 mercerized cotton yarn (see page 170)
Hook size 6 or hook size required to achieve gauge
Approx. 24 in. x 12 in. (60cm x 30cm) satin fabric for lining
2 yd. (2m) satin ribbon, 1½ in. (3.5cm) wide
Size #10 sharp needle and cotton thread

## TECHNIQUES USED
Single and double crochet and cluster stitch (see pattern)

For single crochet: see page 14

For double crochet: see page 16

## GAUGE
This case has a gauge of 3 pattern repeats to 3½ in. (9cm) and 8 rows to 4 in. (10cm) measured over stitch pattern using a G/6 hook, or hook size required to achieve gauge.

## METHOD
### Cluster stitch
**Cluster:** Work [yarn over hook, insert hook, yarn over hook, draw loop through, yarn over hook, draw through 2 loops] over the number of stitches indicated, yarn over hook, draw through all loops on hook.

**Row 1 (wrong side):** 1sc into 2nd chain from hook, 1sc into next chain, * skip 3 chain, 7dc into next chain, skip 3 chain, 1sc into each of next 3 chain, repeat from * to last 4 chain, skip 3 chain, 4dc into last chain. Turn.

**Row 2:** Chain 1, 1sc into 1st stitch, 1sc into next stitch, * chain 3, 1 cluster over next 7 stitches, chain 3, 1sc into each of next 3 stitches, repeat from * to last 4 stitches, chain 3, 1 cluster over last 4 stitches, skip turning chain. Turn.

**Row 3:** Chain 3 [count as 1dc], 3dc into 1st stitch, * skip 3 chain, 1sc into each of next 3sc, skip 3 chain, 7dc into loop which closed next cluster, repeat from * to end finishing with skip 3 chain, 1sc into each of last 2sc, skip turning chain. Turn.

**Row 4:** Chain 3 [count as 1dc], skip 1st stitch, 1 cluster over next 3 stitches, * chain 3, 1sc into each of next 3 stitches, chain 3, 1 cluster over next 7 stitches, repeat from * finishing with chain 3, 1sc into next stitch,

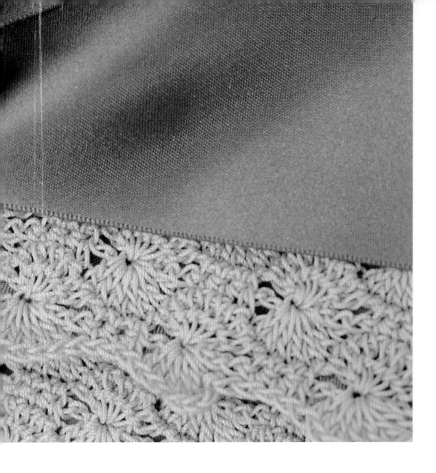

1sc into top of turning chain. Turn.
**Row 5:** Chain 1, 1sc into each of 1st 2sc, * skip 3 chain, 7dc into loop which closed next cluster, skip 3 chain, 1sc into each of next 3sc, repeat from * ending skip 3 chain, 4dc into top of turning chain. Turn.
Repeat Rows 2, 3, 4, and 5.

### Lingerie Case

**Foundation chain:** Make 97 chain.
Follow the Cluster stitch 4-row repeat pattern until work measures 22 in. (56cm) or desired length, finishing on a Row 5.

### TO MAKE UP THE CASE

With right sides together, fold in 7 in. (18cm) at one end to make the pocket, leaving 7½ in. (19cm) to create the flap. Pin and baste the two side seams. Hand stitch using small, neat running stitches. Turn right side out.

Lay a length of ribbon all the way around the case, approx. 2½ in. (6cm) from the left edge. Fold the ribbon over the inside pocket edge (this will be hidden by the lining).

On the outside flap, stop the ribbon just short of the scalloped edge and neatly finish it by turning the end under (this will be hidden by the bow). Pin or baste in position. Secure the short ends of the ribbon using small, neat whip stitches.

### TO MAKE THE LINING

Cut a piece of lining fabric to the same size as the crocheted case, adding a ¾-in. (1.5-cm) seam allowance all the way around.

With right sides together, fold in 7¾ in. (19.5cm) at one end to make the pocket, leaving 7 in. (17.5cm) to create the flap. Pin and baste the two side seams. Stitch.

Turn under ¾-in. (1.5-cm) on each unhemmed edge of the lining and press.

Insert the lining into the crocheted case and pin or baste in position. Stitch the lining to the crocheted case around the pocket opening and flap using small, neat whip stitches.

### TO FINISH

Take a length of satin ribbon and tie it into a large bow. Place the bow on top of the ribbon sash, just above the scalloped edge. Pin or baste in position. Secure with small, neat whip stitches.

# Lacy Pillowcase Edgings

Decorate vintage, heirloom, or crisp new pillowcases and sheets with these very easy lace edgings to create a personal touch to any bedroom. There are three—a pretty lace, a little point, and an ornate scallop shell. They are worked in strips that are then sewn in place, so they are very easy to make. These are made in pristine white mercerized cotton; however, they would look very pretty in soft colors used to enhance faded old pillowcases, perhaps handed down from your grandmother or discovered in your favorite thrift store.

Lace edging                                Scallop-shell edging

# Making the Lacy Pillowcase Edgings

**SIZE**

To fit pillowcases approx. 31½ in. (80cm) long by 19¾ in. (50cm) wide, but measurements can be easily adjusted as required

**MATERIALS**

Approx. 1¾ oz. (50g) Yeoman Yarns Cotton Cannele or similar 4-ply mercerized cotton yarn (see page 170) each for the Lace Edging and the Lace-point Edging and approx. 3¾ oz. (100g) for the Scallop-shell Edging

Hook size B/1

Size #10 sharp needle and cotton thread

**TECHNIQUES USED**

Single crochet and double crochet

| For single crochet: see page 14 |
|---|
| For double crochet: see page 16 |

**TIP**

**Gauge:** Don't worry about gauge too much! Because these edgings are made in strips, you can work extra stitches until the edging is the desired size.

## Lace edging

**GAUGE**

This edging has a gauge of 3 pattern repeats to 2¾ in. (7cm), but working to an exact gauge is not essential (see Tip).

**METHOD**

**Foundation chain:** Chain 11.

**Foundation row:** 2dc in 7th chain from hook, 3 chain, 2dc in next chain, skip next 2 chain, 1dc in last chain. Turn.

**Row 1:** Chain 5, 2dc 3 chain 2dc in 3 chain space. Turn.

**Row 2:** Chain 6, 2dc 3 chain 2dc in 3 chain space, 2 chain, 1dc in 3rd of 5 chain. Turn. Repeat rows 1 and 2 until work measures 31½ in. (80cm) or length required, ending with a Row 1. Do not turn.

**Edging:** Chain 3, 1sc in base of last dc, * 3 chain, [1dc, 3 chain] 3 times in 6 chain space at end of row, skip next row end, 1sc in 3 chain space at center of next row, repeat from * to end, omitting 1st 3 chains and 1sc at end of last repeat. Fasten off.

## Scallop-shell edging

### GAUGE
This edging has a gauge of 1 pattern repeat to 2¾ in. (7cm), but working to an exact gauge is not essential (see Tip).

### METHOD
**Foundation chain:** Chain 8 and join length of chain into ring by working a slip stitch into 1st chain made.

**Row 1:** 3 chain, 8dc into ring, 4 chain. Turn.

**Row 2:** 1dc into 2nd dc, [1 chain, 1dc into next stitch] 7 times, 5 chain. Turn.

**Row 3:** 1dc into 1st space, [2 chain, 1dc into next space] 7 times, 6 chain. Turn.

**Row 4:** 1dc into 1st space, [3 chain, 1dc into next space] 7 times, 1 chain. Turn.

**Row 5:** 1sc, 3dc, 1sc into each space, 8 chain. Turn.

**Row 6:** 1sc into center dc of 1st group of 3, 3 chain. Turn.

**Row 7:** 8dc into space, 4 chain. Turn.

**Row 8:** 1dc into 2nd dc, [1 chain, 1dc into next stitch] 7 times, 1sc into center dc of next group of 3 on previous scallop, 5 chain. Turn.

**Row 9:** As Row 3.

**Row 10:** 1dc into 1st space, [3 chain, 1dc into next space] 7 times, 1sc into center dc of next group of 3 on previous scallop, 1 chain. Turn.

Repeat Rows 5 to 10 inclusive until a corner is required, ending with a Row 10.

### Shape corner
**Row 1:** 1sc 3dc 1sc into each space, 6 chain. Turn.

**Row 2:** 1sc into center dc of 1st group of 3, 3 chain. Turn.

**Row 3:** 12dc into space, 4 chain. Turn.

Repeat Row 8, Row 3, and Row 10, working instructions in brackets 11 times

Lace-point edging

instead of 7 in each row.

**Row 7:** 1sc 3dc 1sc into each space, 8 chain. Turn.

This completes the corner.

Repeat Rows 6 to 10 inclusive of shell edge once, then repeat Rows 5 to 10 inclusive until another corner is required.

Continue working in this way until edging is the required length to fit the pillowcase, ending with a Row 5, omitting final 8 chain. Fasten off, leaving a long thread. Join last three clusters worked to the 1st shell worked, as shown at right on page 64.

## Lace-point edging

### GAUGE
This edging has a gauge of 5 pattern repeats to 7 in. (8cm), but working to an exact gauge is not essential (see Tip).

### METHOD
**Foundation chain:** Chain 103.

**Row 1 (right side):** 1sc into 2nd chain from hook, * work point [6 chain, 1sc into 3rd chain from hook, 1dc into each of next 3 chain], skip 3 chain, 1sc into next chain, repeat from * to end.

Fasten off, leaving a long tail of yarn.

To make this edging to the required length to fit the pillowcase, adjust the number of chains in the foundation chain. If it is too long when you have finished working the points, undo the extra ones.

### TO FINISH
Weave any loose ends into the wrong side of the work. Lay the work out flat, then steam and press lightly.

Place the edging around edge of pillowcase, pin, and hand sew into position using small, neat whip stitches.

# Scented Pillow

This scented pillow is the perfect handmade gift: small, simple, and quick to crochet, yet useful and especially pretty. Hang it in a closet, place it in a lingerie drawer, or simply hook it on a door handle. This pillow is made in crisp, fine white cotton and worked in filet crochet and double crochet for contrast, which reveals an organza pillow filled with fragrant dried lavender. The pillow is tied with silk ribbon and set off by a heart-shaped mother-of-pearl button. Personalize your pillow to create something unique for a friend: embroider or bead, edge or embellish, or use rose petals instead of lavender or perhaps try thyme for a change of pace.

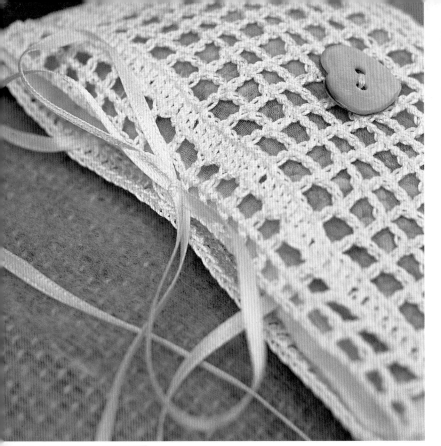

# Making the Scented Pillow

### SIZE
Approx. 6 in. x 4 in. (15cm x 10cm)

### MATERIALS
1 x 1¾ oz. (50g) ball Coats Aida or
similar no. 10 mercerized cotton yarn
(see page 170)
Hook size 6 steel
Button or bead
Fine satin ribbon, ⅛ in. (3mm) wide
Approx. 9 in. (23cm) x 7 in. (18cm) fabric,
such as organza, for pillow form
Size #10 sharp needle and cotton thread
Dried lavender, rose petals, or thyme for
pillow filling

### GAUGE
This pillow has a gauge of 10 stitches and 5
rows to 4 in. (10cm) measured over treble
crochet, but working to an exact gauge is
not essential (see Tips).

### TECHNIQUES USED
Double crochet, filet crochet, and working
with charts (see Tips)

For double crochet: see page 16

### TIPS
**Gauge:** Don't worry about gauge too
much! If your pillow cover ends up a bit
bigger or smaller than the size given here,
just adjust the size of the pillow form.
**Filet crochet charts:** Filet crochet
instructions are usually charted. The blank
squares on the chart represent "spaces" in
the filet, and the squares with a symbol in
them represent the solid "blocks" of
doubles. To follow a filet chart, read the
odd-numbered rows from right to left and
the even-numbered rows from left to right.
From this basic filet technique, many
different patterns can be designed.

### METHOD
**Foundation row:** Leaving a long, loose
end, make 68 chain.
**Row 1:** Work 1dc in 8th chain from hook
to make 1st "space", [2 chain, skip 2 chain
on foundation row, 1dc in next chain]
repeat to end. Turn. [21 spaces in row]
**Row 2:** Make 5 chain, 1dc into top of dc in
row below, [2 chain, 1dc in next dc] repeat
to end, working last dc in 3rd chain of
previous row. Turn.

Continue forming the pattern with "blocks" and "spaces" in this way, following the chart for the pattern, continuing with Row 3 until Row 16 has been completed.

For pillow back, continue to work 16 rows of 1dc in every stitch. [63 stitches] Fasten off.

**To make pillow form**

With wrong sides together, fold fabric in half lengthwise and sew along two sides, using a ¾-in. (1.5-cm) seam allowance. Turn right side out and fill with dried lavender, rose petals, or other scented filling of your choice.

Turn in ends of open side by ¾ in. (1.5cm) and sew with small, neat whip stitches to close.

**TO FINISH**

Weave any loose ends into the wrong side of the work. Lay the work out flat, then steam and press lightly.

With wrong sides together, fold crocheted pillow cover in half lengthwise. Rejoin yarn at one corner and work through both layers, working 2dc into each space and 4dc into each corner, work around three sides of the bag. Fasten off.

Insert scented pillow form.

Add ribbons 3¼ in. (8.5cm) apart and tie bag together with piece of ribbon simply threaded through both sides. Sew on decorative button or bead at the center of pillow front.

KEY

 = block

☐ = space

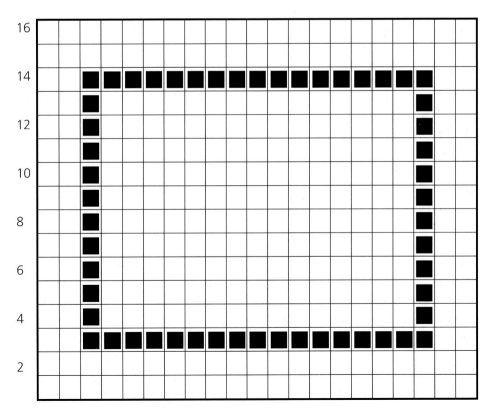

# Filet Lace Pillow

Every beautiful boudoir deserves a pile of sumptuous cushions to add both comfort and glamor.

Worked in patterns of doubles and trebles, this lace cushion, made here in crisp mercerized cotton,

will add a little touch of romance to any bed linen. The lace square is backed with white linen for

timeless appeal, but you could also make it in pastels or summery greens for another room.

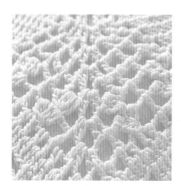

# Making the Filet Lace Pillow

### SIZE
Approx. 16 in. x 16 in. (40cm x 40cm)

### MATERIALS
4 oz. (125g) Yeoman's Cotton Cannele
or similar 4-ply mercerized cotton (see
page 170)
Hook size 1.50mm
Approx. 1 yd. (1m) linen fabric, to back pillow
Size #10 sharp needle and cotton thread in
matching color
16 in. x 16 in. (40cm x 40cm) pillow form

### GAUGE
This pillow has a gauge of 13 rows to 4 in.
(10cm) measured over filet lace pattern, but
working to an exact gauge is not essential
(see Tips).

### TECHNIQUES USED
Single crochet, double crochet, working in
rounds, and cluster stitches (see pattern)

| For single crochet: see page 14 |
| For double crochet: see page 16 |
| For working in rounds: see page 22 |

### TIPS
**Gauge:** Don't worry about gauge too much!
If your pillow cover ends up a bit bigger or
smaller than the size given here, just adjust
the size of the pillow form or continue adding
more rounds until it is the required size.
**Working in rounds:** When you work in
rounds, you never have to turn the fabric.
The right side is always facing you.
**Marking the beginning of a round:**
Mark the beginning of each round with a
coloured thread to make it easier to keep
your place.

### METHOD
#### Cluster stitches
**Double Cluster:** Work a dc into each of
the next 3/5/6 stitches as indicated in the
instructions or as in Round 3 into a 2-chain
space, leaving the last loop of each dc on
the hook. Yarn over hook and draw
through all loops on hook.

**Treble Cluster:** Work a treble into each of
the next 5 stitches or a space, a stitch, and
a space, leaving the last loop of each treble
on the hook. Yarn over hook and draw
through all loops on hook.

**Base ring:** Chain 6 and join length of chain into ring by working a slip stitch into 1st chain made.

**Round 1:** Chain 3 (count as 1dc), work 15dc into ring, slip stitch to 3rd chain.

**Round 2:** Chain 5 (count as 1dc, 2 chain), [1dc into next dc, 2 chain] 15 times, slip stitch to 3rd chain.

**Round 3:** Slip stitch into 1st 2 chain space, [3 double cluster, 3 chain] in every space, slip stitch to top of 1st double cluster.

**Round 4:** Slip stitch into 1st 3-chain space, 5 chain (count as 1dc, 2 chain), [1dc into top of double cluster, 2 chain, 1dc into next 3-chain space, 2 chain] repeat to end. Join with slip stitch to 3rd chain. [32 spaces]

**Round 5:** Slip stitch into 1st 2 chain space, 3 chain (count as 1st dc), 2 more dc in 1st space [3dc in each following space] repeat to end. Join with slip stitch to 3rd chain. [96 dc]

**Round 6:** Chain 5 (count as 1st dc, 2 chain) * skip 1dc, 1dc, 2 chain, skip 1dc, 4dc, 1 chain, skip 1dc, 4dc, 2 chain, repeat from * to end. Join with slip stitch to 3rd chain.

**Round 7:** Chain 6 (count as 1st dc, 3 chain), [1dc, 3 chain] twice, * skip next dc, 5 double cluster over next 5 stitches (count chain space as one stitch), 3 chain, skip next dc, [1dc, 3 chain] 3 times, repeat from * working only 1dc, 3 chain at end of last repeat at end of round. Join with slip stitch to 3rd chain.

**Round 8:** Chain 3 (count as 1st dc), * 3dc in 1st space, * 1dc in next dc, [4dc in next space] twice, 1dc in next dc, [3dc in next space] twice, repeat from * to end of round. Join with slip stitch to 3rd chain.

**Round 9:** Chain 6 (count as 1dc, 3 chain), skip 2dc, 6dc, 1 chain, * 6dc, 3 chain, ** skip 1dc, 1dc between next 2 dc, 3 chain, skip 1dc, 6dc, 1 chain, repeat from

* ending last repeat with chain 3, join with slip stitch to 3rd of 1st 6 chain.

**Round 10:** Chain 6 (count as 1dc, 3 chain), 1dc in next dc, * chain 3, skip 2dc, 3dc, 1 chain, 3dc, 3 chain, skip 2dc, ** [1dc in next dc, 3 chain] 3 times, repeat from * ending last repeat at **, 1dc, 2 chain. Join with slip stitch to 3rd chain.

**Round 11:** Chain 6 (count as 1dc, 3 chain), [1dc in next dc, 3 chain] twice, * 5 double cluster over next 5 stitches (count chain space as 1 stitch), 3 chain, ** [1dc in next dc, 3 chain] 5 times, repeat from * ending last repeat at **, [1dc in next dc, 3 chain] twice. Join with slip stitch to 3rd chain.

**Round 12:** Slip stitch into 1st space, 3 chain [count as 1 dc], 2dc in same space, * 1dc in next dc, 4dc in next space, 1dc in next dc, 3dc in next space, 1dc in top of cluster, 3dc in next space, 1dc in next dc, 4dc in next space, 1dc in next dc, ** [3dc in next space] twice, repeat from * ending last repeat at **, 3dc in next space. Join with slip stitch to 3rd chain.

**Round 13:** Chain 5 [count as 1 tr], 1tr, 3 chain, 2tr in same place, * skip 2 stitches, 10dc, 1 chain, skip 1 stitch, 10dc, 4 chain, skip 2 stitches, 1sc between next 2 stitches, 4 chain, skip 2 stitches, 10dc, 1 chain, skip 1 stitch, 10dc, skip 2 stitches, ** [2tr, 3 chain, 2tr] between next 2 stitches, repeat from * ending last repeat at **. Join with slip stitch to 4th chain.

**Round 14:** Slip stitch into 3 chain space, 4 chain (count as 1st treble), [2tr, 3 chain, 2tr] in this space, 1 chain, * 1tr between next 2 stitches, skip 2 stitches, 9dc, 1 chain, 9dc, skip 1 stitch, [4 chain, sc in loop] twice, 4 chain, skip 1 stitch, 9dc, 1 chain, 9dc, skip 1 stitch, 1tr between next 2 stitches, 1 chain, ** [2tr, 3 chain, 2tr] in 3

chain loop, 1 chain, repeat from * ending last repeat at **. Join with slip stitch to 4th chain.

**Round 15:** Slip stitch into 3 chain space, 4 chain (count as 1st treble), * [2tr, 3 chain, 2tr] in this space, [1 chain, 1tr between next 2 stitches] twice, skip next 2 stitches, 8dc, 1 chain, 8dc, skip next stitch, [4 chain, sc in next loop] three times, 4 chain, skip 1 stitch, 8dc, 1 chain, 8dc, skip 2 stitches, [1tr between next 2 stitches, 1 chain] twice, repeat from * to end of round. Join with slip stitch to 4th chain.

**Round 16:** Slip stitch into 3 chain space, 4 chain (count as 1st treble), * [2tr, 3 chain, 2tr] in this space, skip 1 stitch, [1 chain, 1tr in next stitch] twice, 1 chain, 1tr in next space, skip next 2 stitches, 14dc, skip 1 stitch, [4 chain, sc in next loop] 4 times, 4 chain, skip next stitch, 14dc, 1 chain, skip 2 stitches, 1tr in next space, 1 chain, [1tr, 1 chain in next stitch] twice, skip next stitch, repeat from * to end of round. Join with slip stitch to 4th chain.

**Round 17:** Slip stitch into 3 chain space, 4 chain [count as 1st treble], * [2tr, 3 chain, 2tr] in this space, skip next stitch, [1 chain, 1tr in next stitch] 3 times, 1 chain, 1tr in next space, skip next 2 stitches, 12dc, skip 1dc, [4 chain, 1sc in next loop] 5 times, 4 chain, skip next stitch, 12dc, skip 2 stitches, 1tr in next space, 1 chain, [1tr, 1 chain in next stitch] 3 times, skip next stitch, repeat from * to end of round. Join with slip stitch to 4th chain.

**Round 18:** Slip stitch into 3 chain space, 4 chain [count as 1st treble], [2tr, 3 chain, 2tr] in this space, skip next stitch, [1 chain, 1tr in next stitch] 4 times, 1 chain, 1tr in next space, skip next 2 stitches, 10dc, skip 1 stitch, [4 chain, 1sc in next loop]

6 times, 4 chain, skip next stitch, 10dc, skip 2 stitches, 1tr in next space, 1 chain, [1tr, 1 chain in next stitch] 4 times, skip next stitch, repeat from * to end of round. Join with slip stitch to 4th chain.

**Round 19:** Slip stitch into 3 chain space, 4 chain [count as 1st treble], * [2tr, 3 chain, 2tr] in this space, 3 chain, skip 2 stitches, 5 treble cluster round next stitch, 3 chain, 1tr in next stitch, 3 chain, skip next stitch, 5 treble cluster round next stitch, 2 chain, 1 treble into same space as cluster, skip 2 stitches, 8dc, skip 1 stitch, [4 chain, 1sc in next loop] 7 times, 4 chain, skip next stitch, 8dc, skip 2 stitches, 1tr in next space, 2 chain, 5tr cluster round next stitch, 3 chain, skip next stitch, 1tr in next stitch, 3 chain, 5 treble cluster round next stitch, 3 chain, repeat from * to end of round. Join with slip stitch to 4th chain.

**Round 20:** Slip stitch into 3 chain space, 4 chain [count as 1st treble], * [2tr, 3 chain, 2tr] in this space, 3 chain, skip 1 stitch, 1tr in next stitch, 3 chain, [5tr cluster over cluster on previous round, 3 chain, 1tr in next stitch, 3 chain] twice, skip next stitch, 6 double cluster over next 6 stitches, 3 chain, skip 1 stitch, [1dc, 1 chain, 1dc, 1 chain in next loop] 8 times, 2 chain, skip 1 stitch, 6 double cluster over next 6 stitches, 3 chain, skip 1 stitch, 1tr in next stitch, 3 chain, [5 treble cluster over cluster on previous round, 3 chain, 1tr in next stitch, 3 chain] twice, skip next stitch, repeat from * to end of round. Join with slip stitch to 4th chain.

**Round 21:** Slip stitch into 3 chain space, 3 chain [count as 1st double], * [2dc, 3 chain, 2dc] into this space, 1 chain, [1dc, 1 chain] between next 2 stitches, [1dc in next space, 1 chain, 1dc in next stitch,

1 chain] 6 times, [1dc in next space, 1 chain] 17 times, [1dc in next stitch, 1 chain, 1dc in next space, 1 chain] 6 times, [1dc between next 2 stitches, 1 chain] repeat from * to end of round. Join with slip stitch to 3rd chain.

**Round 22:** Slip stitch into 3 chain space, 3 chain [count as 1st dc], * [3dc, 3 chain, 3dc] into this space, [2 chain, skip 2 stitches, 3dc] 18 times, skip 2 stitches, repeat from * to end of round, 2 chain, join with slip stitch to 3rd chain.

**Round 23:** Slip stitch into 3 chain space, 3 chain [count as 1st dc], * [3dc, 3 chain, 3dc] into this space, 3dc in next 3dc, [2 chain, 3dc in next 3 dc] to corner, 3dc, repeat from * to end of round. Join with slip stitch to 3rd chain.

**Round 24:** Slip stitch into 3 chain space, 3 chain [count as 1st dc] * [3dc, 3 chain, 3dc] into this space, 2 chain, skip 1st 3 stitches, [3dc in next 3dc, 2 chain] to last 6 dc before corner, 3dc, 2 chain, skip 3 dc, repeat from * to end of round. Join with slip stitch to 3rd chain.

**Round 25:** As Round 23.

**Round 26:** As Round 24.

**Round 27:** Slip stitch into 3 chain space, 3 chain [count as 1st dc], * [3dc, 3 chain, 3dc] into this space, [3dc in each dc, 2dc in each space to corner], repeat from * to end of round. Join with slip stitch to 3rd chain. Fasten off.

### TO MAKE UP

Weave in all yarn ends. Lay work out flat, cover with a fine cloth, and steam gently. Cut the backing fabric to 40¼ in. x 17 in. (101cm x 42.5cm).

Make a hem along each end of the short edges, as follows:

Fold ½ in. (1cm), then 1½ in. (3.5cm) to the wrong side and pin, baste, then topstitch these two hems. Remove the basting and press.

Lay the piece on a flat surface with the right side facing upward and overlap them by 4¾ in. (12cm) so that the cover measures 15¾ in. (39cm) from fold to fold. Pin the open sides together and sew the seams ⅝ in. (1.5cm) from the raw edges. Trim the seams to ¼ in. (0.75cm) and finish the raw edges with a zigzag stitch. Turn pillow cover right sides out and press.

### TO FINISH

Hand stitch the crochet piece to the front of the pillow cover; stitching around the edge of the filet lace square using a size #10 sharp needle and matching cotton thread with small, neat whip stitches.

# Patchwork Throw

Motifs are characteristic of crochet: small and versatile, they take no time to make and can be picked up, put down, even forgotten about for ages and then started up again. At first glance this throw looks a little daunting to make, but it is simply a collection of easy six-sided motifs. Worked in single crochet in two colors, it gives a very effective "spot" design. Take time when considering your color combinations, but don't be too planned. Work as many motifs as you need and sew them together with a simple whip stitch to keep the throw flat. This throw works well in both contemporary and traditional interiors or as a cozy blanket in the car.

# Making the Patchwork Throw

### SIZE
Approx. 65¾ in. x 62½ in. (159cm x 167cm), but measurements can be easily adjusted as required

### MATERIALS
Rowan Cotton Glacé or a similar sport-weight glazed cotton yarn (see page 170) in 12 contrasting colors as follows:

**Color A:** 7 x 1¾ oz. (50g) balls in orange
**Color B:** 7 x 1¾ oz. (50g) balls in hot pink
**Color C:** 7 x 1¾ oz. (50g) balls in olive
**Color D:** 7 x 1¾ oz. (50g) balls in dark green
**Color E:** 7 x 1¾ oz. (50g) balls in pale pink
**Color F:** 7 x 1¾ oz. (50g) balls in light blue
**Color G:** 7 x 1¾ oz. (50g) balls in lilac
**Color H:** 7 x 1¾ oz. (50g) balls in purple
**Color I:** 7 x 1¾ oz. (50g) balls in gray
**Color J:** 7 x 1¾ oz. (50g) balls in yellow
**Color K:** 7 x 1¾ oz. (50g) balls in plum
**Color L:** 7 x 1¾ oz. (50g) balls in fuchsia
Hook size D/3
Large sewing needle

### TECHNIQUES USED
Double crochet and working in rounds

For double crochet: see page 16

For working in rounds: see page 22

### GAUGE
Each hexagonal motif measures 4 in. (10cm) in diameter when worked in double crochet over five rounds.

### TIPS
**Gauge:** Don't worry about gauge too much! Because these motifs are made in rounds, you can work your stitches in a circle until the motif is the required size.

**Working in rounds:** When you work in rounds, you never have to turn the fabric. The right side is always facing you.

**Marking the beginning of a round:** Mark the beginning of each round to make it easier to keep your place.

**Joining in a new yarn:** Begin the last double crochet in the usual way, but change to the new yarn when drawing the yarn through to the last loop of the stitch. Leave a long, loose end of the old and new yarns to weave in later, or work over the ends for several stitches before clipping them off.

**Yarns:** You can use up odd balls of yarn to make this throw. Since it is made up of lots

of small motifs, mixed dye lots do not matter. End of line colors, often from the sale bin or remnants from your own stash, can make a great throw in the age-old tradition of grandmother's patchwork flower garden.

## METHOD
### Hexagonal motif
**Base ring:** Leaving a long, loose end and using first color, make 4 chain and join length of chain into ring by working a slip stitch into 1st chain made.

**Round 1:** Chain 3 [counts as 1dc], 1dc into ring, [1 chain, 2dc into ring] 5 times, 1 chain, slip stitch to top of 3 chain. [6 spaces]

**Round 2:** Slip stitch into next dc and into next chain, 3 chain [counts as 1dc], * 1dc in next 2dc **, work a V stitch of 1dc 1 chain 1dc into next space, repeat from * 4 times and from * to ** once, 1dc into last space, 1 chain, slip stitch to top of 3 chain.

Change to second color.

**Round 3:** Chain 3 [counts as 1dc], 1dc in each dc and 1 V stitch into each space all around, slip stitch to top of 3 chain. [6 groups of 6dc]

**Round 4:** As round 3. [6 groups of 8dc]

**Round 5:** As round 3. [6 groups of 10dc]
Fasten off.

This completes one motif. Work the number of motifs required in combinations of any two colors of your choice.

For the size of throw shown here, 295 motifs are required.

## TO FINISH
Weave any loose ends into the wrong side of each motif. Lay the work out flat, then steam and press lightly.

Lay the motifs out flat, alternating rows of 16 motifs and rows of 15 motifs. Join together with strands of colored yarn using small, neat whip stitches.

Using the color of your choice, rejoin the yarn and work a row of dc around the entire edge of the throw, working a V stitch into each V stitch and working 2dc together where the motifs join to keep the throw flat.

# Contemporary

Simple textures and free-form organic structures are the perfect foils to bold, modern décor. Add a new dimension by contrasting the handmade with the hard-edged. Wood, glass, plastic, and ceramic in contemporary interiors can be softened by silky cotton, whisper-fine mohair, wool, and sumptuous cashmere. Such projects as the spider's web drape, table runner, and comfortable pillows create a distinctive and updated statement, especially when done in simple black and white.

# Spider's Web Drape

A twist on a traditional lace drape, this window panel is worked in whisper-fine mohair with a metallic shimmer. The drape is trimmed with random, asymmetrical crochet motifs and further decorated with sequins for a touch of glamour.

 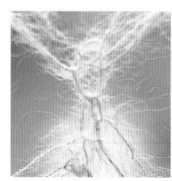 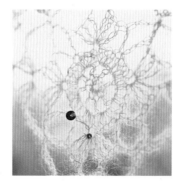

# Making the Spider's Web Drape

### SIZE
Approx. 98 in. x 47 in. (250cm x 120cm), but size can be easily adjusted as required

### MATERIALS
5 x 1 oz. (25g) balls Rowan Kidsilk Haze or similar lightweight mohair yarn (see page 170)
Hook sizes C/2 and H/8
Sequins, if desired

### TECHNIQUES USED
Solomon's Knot stitch

For Solomon's Knot: see page 21

### GAUGE
This drape has a gauge of 5 stitches and 7 rows to 8 in. (20cm) measured over Solomon's Knot pattern using a H/8 hook.

### TIPS
**Gauge:** Don't worry about gauge too much! Because this drape is made in multiples, you can work extra stitches until the drape is the required size.
**Edge Solomon's Knot (ESK):** These form the base "chain" and edges of the fabric and are only two-thirds the length of the Main Solomon's Knot.
**Main Solomon's Knot (MSK):** These form the main fabric and are a little longer than the Edge Solomon's Knot.

### METHOD
**Foundation "chain":** Using H/8 hook, work 2 chain, 1sc into 2nd chain from hook, now make 52ESK and 1MSK.
**Row 1:** 1sc into sc between 3rd and 4th loops from hook, * 2MSK, skip 2 loops, 1sc into next sc, repeat from * to end.
**Row 2:** 2ESK, 1MSK, 1sc into sc between 4th and 5th loops from hook, * 2MSK, skip 2 loops, 1sc into next sc, repeat from * ending in top of ESK.

Repeat Row 2 until work measures 98 in. (250cm) or required length.

### Square motif
**Base ring:** Using H/8 hook, chain 4 and join length of chain into ring by working a slip stitch into 1st chain made.
**Round 1:** Work 8sc into circle, slip stitch to 1st sc.
**Round 2:** Chain 4, 1dc into next sc, * 1 chain, 1dc into next sc, repeat from * ending 1 chain, slip stitch into 3rd of

4 chain. [8 chain spaces]

**Round 3:** Chain 3, 3dc into 1 chain space, * 1dc into 1dc, 3dc into 1 chain space, repeat from * ending slip stitch into 3rd of 3 chain. [31dc]

**Round 4:** Chain 9, treble into same place as slip stitch, * skip 3dc, 3tr 5 chain 3tr into next dc, skip 3dc, 1tr 5 chain 1tr into next dc, repeat from * ending slip stitch into 4th of 9 chain.

**Round 5:** Slip stitch to center of 5 chain, 1sc into space, 7 chain, ** 3tr 5 chain 3tr into 5 chain space, 7 chain, sc into 5 chain space, 7 chain, repeat from ** ending slip stitch into 1st sc. Fasten off.

### Star motif

**Base ring:** Using H/8 hook, chain 6 and join length of chain into ring by working a slip stitch into 1st chain made.

**Round 1:** Chain 1, [1sc into ring, 3 chain] 12 times, slip stitch to 1st sc.

**Round 2:** Slip stitch into each of next 2 chain, 1 chain, 1sc into same 3 chain arch, [3 chain, 1sc into next 3 chain arch] 11 times, 1 chain, 1 half-double into top of 1st sc.

**Round 3:** * chain 6, 1sc into next 3 chain arch **, chain 3, 1sc into next 3 chain arch, repeat from * 4 times and from * to ** once, chain 1, 1dc into half-double that closed previous round.

**Round 4:** * [5dc, 2 chain, 5dc] into next 6 chain arch, 1sc into next 3 chain arch, repeat from * 5 times ending last repeat in dc that closed previous round, slip stitch into next stitch. Fasten off.

### Double-star motif

**Base ring:** Wind yarn 7 times round little finger to form a circle, and using H/8 hook, slip stitch into circle to secure.

**Round 1:** Chain 3, 3dc into circle, [9 chain,

4dc into circle] 5 times, 9 chain, slip stitch into top of 1st 3 chain.

**Round 2:** Slip stitch into 1st dc, * 1sc into next dc, [9dc, 2 chain, 9dc] into next 9 chain loop, skip next 2dc, repeat from * 5 times, slip stitch into 1st sc. Turn.

**Round 3:** Slip stitch into each of 1st 4dc, * 1sc into each of next 5dc, 2sc into next 2 chain loop, 1sc into each of next 5dc, 2 chain, skip next 8dc, repeat from * 5 times, slip stitch to 1st sc. Fasten off.

### Webbed-star motif

**Base ring:** Using H/8 hook, chain 8 and join length of chain into ring by working a slip stitch into 1st chain made.

**Round 1:** [chain 14, 1sc into 7th chain from hook, 7 chain, 1sc into circle] 7 times, 14 chain, 1sc into 7th chain from hook, yarn round hook 6 times, insert hook into circle, yarn round hook and draw through a loop, [yarn round hook and draw through first 2 loops on hook] 6 times, yarn round hook and draw through remaining two loops on hook.

**Round 2:** * Chain 5, [1sc, 5 chain] 4 times into next 6 chain loop, 1sc into same loop, repeat from * 7 times. Fasten off.

### Small-circle motif

**Base ring:** Wind yarn 8 times round little finger to form a circle, and using C/2 hook, slip stitch into circle to secure.

**Round 1:** Chain 1, 20sc into ring, slip stitch to 1st sc. Fasten off.

### Small-flowers motif

**Base ring:** Wind yarn 8 times round little finger to form a circle, and using C/2 hook, slip stitch into circle to secure.

**Round 1:** Chain 1, 20sc into ring, slip stitch to 1st sc.

**Round 2:** [Chain 3, 1sc into next sc, skip next sc] repeat all round. Fasten off.

### Large round motif

**Base ring:** Using H/8 hook, work rounds 1 to 7 inclusive of motif given for String Ottoman (see pages 56–7).

### Small round motif

**Base ring:** Using C/2 hook, make 4 chain and join length of chain into ring by working a slip stitch into 1st chain made.

**Round 1:** 8sc into ring, slip stitch into 1st sc.

**Round 2:** Chain 4, 1 treble into same place as slip stitch, [3 chain, 2 treble into next sc] repeat all around, ending 3 chain, slip stitch into 4th of 4 chain. Fasten off.

### Six-petal flower motif

**Base ring:** Wind yarn 10 times round little finger to form a circle, and using C/2 hook, work 30sc into ring.

**Round 1:** 1sc into each sc, join with slip stitch to 1st sc.

**Round 2:** 1sc into next sc, * 12 chain, 1sc into each of next 5sc, repeat from * ending with 12 chain, 1sc into each of next 4sc, slip stitch into 1st sc.

**Round 3:** * Into next 12 chain loop work 2sc 2 half-double 9dc 2 half-double 2sc, skip 1sc, 1sc into each of next 3sc, repeat from * to end.

**Round 4:** * Work 1sc into each of next 17 stitches, skip 1sc, slip stitch into next sc, skip 1sc, repeat from * to end. Fasten off.

### TO FINISH

Lay the work out flat and arrange the motifs at the bottom edge of the drape as desired. Attach lightly with the same yarn. Adorn with as many or as few sequins as you prefer.

# Molded Wire Mat

When worked in wire, crochet takes on a whole new appearance. This is a very distinctive piece to crochet. Soft wire in blues, violets, bronze, and turquoise are made into simple motifs in various sizes and assembled in a very free-form way to create a twist on the traditional table runner. They are attached and filled in with random chains of crochet, twisted, and scrunched to produce an unusual, yet very decorative piece for a table with a very individual look.

# Making the Molded Wire Mat

### SIZE
Approx. 11 in. x 14 in. (28cm x 36cm), but size can be easily adjusted as required

### MATERIALS
Assorted reels of 24-gauge (0.5mm-) colored artistic wire, (available from good craft stores) Hook size G/6

### TECHNIQUES USED
Single crochet and working in rounds

For single crochet: see page 14

For working in rounds: see page 22

### GAUGE
Each large circular motif measures approx. 2 in. (5cm) in diameter when worked in single crochet using a G/6 hook.

### TIPS
**Gauge:** Don't worry about gauge too much! Because these motifs are made in rounds, you can work your stitches in circles until it is the required size.

**Working in rounds:** When you work in rounds, you never have to turn the fabric. The right side is always facing you.

### METHOD
#### Large circular motif
**Base ring:** Wind wire 4 times round little finger to form a circle, and using G/6 hook, work 16sc into ring, slip stitch to 1st sc.

**Next round:** Chain 1, 1sc in same place as turning chain, work 2sc in each sc to end. Join with slip stitch to chain. Fasten off, leaving 6-in. (15-cm) length of wire to join motifs.

#### Small circular motifs
Work as Large circular motif, but fasten off after 16sc have been worked.

### TO FINISH
Sketch a diagram of where you want to place each motif. Using any color wire and any long ends, join the motifs to form the outer edge. Refer to your diagram to make sure they are in the correct position. Join the motifs with a few chain stitches, cut the wire, and fasten off by pushing the ends of the wire through the work. Fill in by crocheting short chains with a long piece of wire either end and use these as links—pushing the wires through the edges of the circles. Make sure that your work is lying flat, or scrunch as you go for more decorative effect.

# Round Rose Pillow Cover

This crochet pillow is an intriguing change from the conventional square pillow shape. Worked in rounds to form petal shapes, the cover can be made to fit any size round pillow form. The contemporary black-and-white combination could be given a modern country look if made in string, with a floral-print fabric underneath.

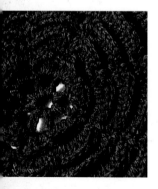

# Making the Round Rose Pillow Cover

Approx. 15 in. (38cm) diameter, but size can be easily adjusted as required

## MATERIALS
4 x 1¾ oz. (50g) balls Rowan Classic Cashwool or similar sport-weight wool yarn (see page 170)
Hook size D/3
Tapestry needle
Circular pillow form, 15 in. (38cm) diameter

## TECHNIQUES USED
Single, double, half-double, and treble crochet and working in rounds

For single crochet: see page 14
For double crochet: see page 16
For half-double crochet: see page 18
For treble crochet: see page 19
For working in rounds: see page 22

## GAUGE
This pillow has a gauge of 5 rounds to 3¼ in. (8.5cm) measured over pattern using a D/3 hook, but working to an exact gauge is not essential (see Tips).

## TIPS
**Gauge:** Don't worry about gauge too much! Because this pillow cover is made in rounds, you can work your stitches in circles until it is the required size.
**Working in rounds:** When you work in rounds, you never have to turn the fabric. The right side is always facing you.
**Marking the beginning of a round:** Mark the beginning of each round to make it easier to keep your place.

## METHOD
### Front and Back (make 2)
**Base ring:** Chain 6 and join length of chain into ring by working a slip stitch into 1st chain made.
**Round 1:** Chain 5 [1dc, 2 chain] 7 times into ring, slip stitch to 3rd of 5 chain. [8 spaces]
**Round 2:** Into each space work [1sc, 1 half-double, 3dc, 1 half-double, 1sc], slip stitch into 1st sc. [8 petals]
**Round 3:** [chain 4, 1sc between next 2 petals] to end.
**Round 4:** Into each loop work [1sc, 1 half-double, 5dc, 1 half-double, 1sc], slip stitch to 1st sc.
**Round 5:** [chain 6, 1sc between next 2 petals] to end.
**Round 6:** Into each loop work [1sc, 1 half-double, 7dc, 1 half-double, 1sc] slip stitch to 1st sc.
**Round 7:** [chain 8, 1sc between next 2 petals] to end.
**Round 8:** Into each loop work [1sc, 1 half-double, 9dc, 1 half-double, 1sc], slip stitch to 1st sc.
**Round 9:** [chain 10, 1sc between next 2 petals] to end.
**Round 10:** Into each loop work [1sc, 1 half-double, 11dc, 1 half-double, 1sc], slip stitch to 1st sc.
**Round 11:** [chain 12, 1sc between next 2 petals] to end.
**Round 12:** Into each loop work [1sc, 1 half-double, 13dc, 1 half-double, 1sc], slip stitch to 1st sc.
**Round 13:** [chain 14, 1sc between next 2 petals] to end.

**Round 14:** Into each loop work [1sc, 1 half-double, 15dc, 1 half-double, 1sc], slip stitch to 1st sc.
**Round 15:** [chain 16, 1sc between next 2 petals] to end.
**Round 16:** Into each loop work [1sc, 1 half-double, 17dc, 1 half-double, 1sc], slip stitch to 1st sc.
**Round 17:** [chain 9, 1sc behind center dc on next petal, chain 9, 1sc between next 2 petals], repeat to end.
**Round 18:** Into each loop work [1sc, 1 half-double, 9dc, 1 half-double, 1sc] in each 9 chain space, slip stitch to 1st dc.
**Round 19:** [chain 10, 1sc between next 2 petals] to end.
**Round 20:** Into each loop work [1sc, 1 half-double, 10dc, 1 half-double, 1sc] in each space, slip stitch to 1st sc.
**Round 21:** [chain 11, 1sc between next 2 petals] to end.
**Round 22:** Into each loop work [1sc, 1 half-double, 11dc, 1 half-double, 1sc] in each space, slip stitch to 1st sc.
**Round 23:** [chain 12, 1sc between next 2 petals] to end.
**Round 24:** Into each loop work [1sc, 1 half-double, 12dc, 1 half-double, 1sc] in each space, slip stitch to 1st sc.
**Round 25:** Chain 4, [skip 1st sc and half-double, work 1dc in each of next 12dc, skip next half-double and sc, work 1 treble between petals] repeat to end, slip stitch to top of 4 chain.
**Round 26:** Chain 3, 1dc in each stitch to end. Fasten off.

## TO FINISH

Weave any loose ends into the wrong side of the work. Lay the work out flat, then steam and press lightly.

Place the pieces together with wrong sides facing and pin. Oversew the edge using yarn and a tapestry needle until the opening is just large enough to insert the pillow form. Finish sewing the edge to enclose the pillow form. Fasten off and weave in any yarn ends.

# Appliqué Flower Pillow

This is a very easy, yet effective home accessory. Simple crochet motifs are sewn onto a knitted pillow cover for contrast. Make the motifs in contrasting colors and decorate the pillows with French knots or beads.

 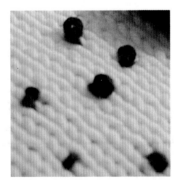

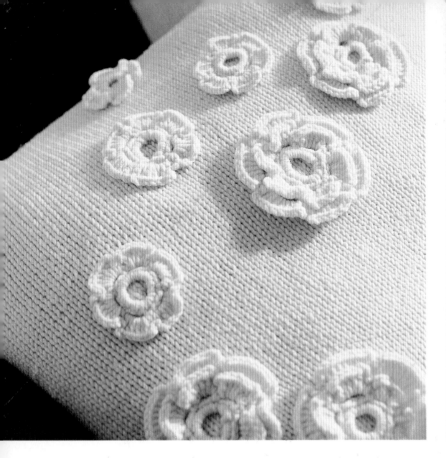

# Making the Appliqué Flower Pillow

## SIZE

Small, medium, and large flowers to be
appliquéd onto the pillow of your choice—
the pillows shown here are 16 in. x 16 in.
(40cm x 40cm)

## MATERIALS

1 x 1¾ oz. (50g) ball Jaeger DK Merino or a
similar sport-weight yarn (see page 170)
will make 4 large, 4 medium, and 4 small
flower motifs
Hook sizes B/1 and D/3
Tapestry needle

## TECHNIQUES USED

Single and double crochet, and working in
rounds

| For single crochet: see page 14 |
| --- |
| For double crochet: see page 16 |
| For working in rounds: see page 22 |

## GAUGE

The motifs should measure approx.
3 in. (7.5cm) for the large size, 2½ in.
(6.5cm) for the medium size, and 2 in.
(5cm) for the small size, but working to an
exact gauge is not essential (see Tips).

## TIPS

**Gauge:** Don't worry about gauge too
much! Because these flower motifs are
made in rounds, you can work your stitches
in a circle until it is the required size.

**Working in rounds:** When you work in
rounds, you never have to turn the fabric.
The right side is always facing you.

## METHOD

### Large rose

**Base ring:** Using a hook size D/3, make 12
chain and join length of chain into ring by
working a slip stitch into 1st chain made.

**Round 1 (right side):** Chain 1, work 18sc
into ring, join with a slip stitch into 1st sc.

**Round 2:** Chain 1, 1sc into same stitch as
chain, 3ch, skip 2 stitches [1sc in next
stitch, 3ch, skip 2 stitches] 5 times,
slip stitch to 1st sc.

**Round 3:** Chain 1, [in next 3ch loop work
a petal of 1sc, 3ch, 5dc, 3ch, 1sc] 6 times,

slip stitch to 1st sc.

**Round 4:** Chain 1, [1sc between 2sc, 5 chain behind petal of round 3] 6 times, slip stitch to 1st sc.

**Round 5:** Chain 1, [in next 5ch loop work a petal of 1sc, 3ch, 7dc, 3ch, 1sc] 6 times, slip stitch to 1st sc. Fasten off, leaving a long tail of yarn.

### Medium rose

Work as given for Large rose, working Rounds 1 to 3 inclusive.

### Small rose

Using hook size B/1, work as given for Medium rose.

### TO FINISH

Weave any loose ends into the wrong side of the work.

Pin flowers randomly onto your chosen pillow and then sew into position. If desired, further embellish the pillow with French knots.

**French knot embroidery:** To make a French knot, bring the yarn out at the required position, hold the yarn down where it emerges with the left thumb, and encircle the thread twice with the needle. Still holding the thread firmly with your thumb, twist the needle back to the starting point and insert it close to where the thread first emerged (not in the exact place or it will simply pull back through). Pull the needle through to the back, leaving a small knot on the surface, or pass on to the position of the next stitch.

### Making a knitted pillow

### PILLOW SIZE

Pillow cover is approx. 15¾ in. x 15¾ in (40cm x 40cm)

### MATERIALS

6 x 1¾ oz. (50g) balls Jaeger Extra Fine Merino or a similar sports-weight yarn (see page 170)
1 pair each of no. 10 and no. 8 size knitting needles
Sewing needle
16 in. x 16 in. (40cm x 40cm) pillow form
5 buttons, approx. ¾ in. (2cm) diameter

### GAUGE

22 stitches and 32 rows to 4 in. (10cm) over stockinette stitch on no. 8 size needles.

### METHOD
### Back

With no. 8 needles, cast on 90 stitches and work 16 in. (40cm) in stockinette stitch— knit 1 row, purl 1 row alternately—finishing with a purl row (wrong side).

### Button band

Starting with a knit row, work 10 rows in stockinette stitch.

**Next row (right side):** Change to no. 10 needles, purl to end.

**Next row (wrong side):** Change to no. 8 needles, purl to end.

Starting with a knit row, work 9 more rows in stockinette stitch. Bind off.

### Front

With no. 8 needles, cast on 90 stitches and work 16 in. (40cm) in stockinette stitch— knit 1 row, purl 1 row alternately—finishing with a purl row (wrong side).

### Buttonhole band

Starting with a knit row, work 4 rows in stockinette stitch.

**Row 5 (buttonhole):** Knit 8 stitches, bind off next 3 stitches, [knit until 15 stitches on right-hand needle after last bind off, bind off next 3 stitches] 4 times, knit to end.

**Row 6:** Purl across row, casting on 3 stitches over those bound off in previous row.

Work 4 more rows in stockinette stitch, finishing with a purl row.

**Next row (right side):** Change to no. 10 needles; purl to end.

**Next row (wrong side):** Change to no. 8 needles; purl to end.

Starting with a knit row, work 3 more rows in stockinette stitch.

Repeat Rows 5 and 6.

Work 4 more rows in stockinette stitch. Bind off.

### TO FINISH

Weave any loose ends into the wrong side of the work. Lay the pieces out flat, then steam and press lightly.

Pin back and front pieces with right sides together. Use a small neat backstitch to join three sides, leaving the buttonhole band open.

Next fold the button bands in half along the purl stitch row and sew to the inside.

Turn pillow cover right side out and sew on the buttons to correspond with the buttonholes.

Insert the pillow form and button up.

# Round Floor Rug

A playful twist on traditional crochet, a round floor, or "doily," rug for the floor, is perfect for adding a bit of warmth, texture, and color to any room. Quick to make, this project can be created over a weekend for instant, practical glamour. Made in thick yarn on a small hook to give a felted appearance, this rug could just as easily be created from remnants of several different yarns for a country look. It would make a very attractive addition to a boudoir if worked in strips of floral-print cotton, satin ribbon, or maybe even fine leather. Alternatively, try it in natural string to add a little homespun chic.

# Making the Round Floor Rug

### SIZE
Approx. 36 in. (92cm) diameter, but size can be easily adjusted as required

### MATERIALS
7 x 3¾ oz. (100g) balls Rowan Big Wool or similar fat wool yarn (see page 170)
Hook size L/10½

### TECHNIQUES USED
Single and double crochet, and working in rounds

For single crochet: see page 14

For double crochet: see page 16

For working in rounds: see page 22

### GAUGE
Working to an exact gauge is not essential (see Tips).

### TIPS
**Gauge:** Don't worry about gauge too much! Because this rug is made in rounds, you can work your stitches in circles until it is the required size.

**Working in rounds:** When you work in rounds, you never have to turn the fabric. The right side is always facing you.

**Marking the beginning of a round:** Mark the beginning of each round to make it easier to keep your place.

### METHOD
**Base ring:** Chain 9 and join length of chain into ring by working a slip stitch into 1st chain made.

**Round 1:** Chain 3, 17dc into ring, slip stitch into top of 3 chain.

**Round 2:** Chain 3, 1dc 2 chain 2dc into same stitch as 3 chain, * 1 chain, skip 2dc, 2dc 2 chain 2dc into next dc, repeat from * all round, finish with 1 chain, skip 2dc, slip stitch into top of 3 chain.

**Round 3:** Slip stitch into 1dc and into space, 3 chain, 1dc 2 chain 2dc into same space as slip stitch, * 1 chain 1dc into next space, 1 chain, 2dc 2 chain 2dc into next space, repeat from * all round, finish with 1 chain, 1dc into space, 1 chain, slip stitch into top of 3 chain.

**Round 4:** Slip stitch into 1dc and into space, 3 chain, 1dc 2 chain 2dc into same space as slip stitch, * 1 chain 1dc into next space, 2 chain 1dc into next space, 1 chain 2dc 2 chain 2dc into next space, repeat from * all round, finish 1 chain 1dc into next space, 2 chain 1dc into next space, chain 1, slip stitch into top of 3 chain.

**Round 5:** Slip stitch into dc and into space, 3 chain 1dc 2 chain 2dc into space, * 1 chain 1dc into next space, 1 chain 5dc into next space, 1 chain 1dc into next space, 1 chain 2dc 2 chain 2dc into next space, repeat from* all round, finish with 1 chain 1dc into space, 1 chain 5dc into next space, 1 chain 1dc into next space, 1 chain, slip stitch into top of 3 chain.

**Round 6:** Slip stitch into dc and into space, 3 chain 1dc 2 chain 2dc into space, * 1 chain 1dc into next space, 1 chain, skip 1 space, 2dc into next dc, 1dc into each of next 3dc, 2dc into next dc, 1 chain, skip 1 space, 1dc into next space, 1 chain 2dc 2 chain 2dc into next space, repeat from * all round, finish with 1 chain 1dc into next space, 1 chain, skip 1 space, 2dc into next double, 1dc into each of next 3dc, 2dc into next dc, 1 chain, skip 1 space, 1dc into next space, 1 chain, slip stitch into top of 3 chain.

**Round 7:** As Round 6, working 2dc into each dc, 1dc into each of the next 5dc, 2dc into dc.

Continue working the extra dc until there are 21dc in each group of dc.

**Round 14:** Slip stitch into dc, 1sc into space, * 5 chain, skip 1 space, 3dc into next space, 2 chain, skip 1dc, 1dc into each of the next 19dc, 2 chain, 3dc into next space, 5 chain, skip 1 space, 1sc into next space, repeat from * all round, finish with 5 chain, slip stitch into 1st sc.

**Round 15:** Slip stitch into 2 chain, 1sc into space, * 5 chain, 3dc into next space, 2 chain, skip 1dc, 1dc into each of next 17dc, 2 chain, 3dc into next space, [5 chain 1sc] into each of next 2 spaces, repeat from * all round, finish with 5 chain, slip stitch into 1st sc.

Continue as last round, working 2dc less in each group of dc and [5 chain 1sc] into extra space on each round until 7 stitches remain.

**Next round:** Slip stitch into 2 chain, 1sc into space, * 5 chain, 3dc into next space, 2 chain, skip 1dc, leaving last loop of each dc on hook, 1dc into each of next 5dc, draw yarn through remaining stitches, 2 chain, 3dc into space, [5 chain 1sc] into each of next 8 spaces, repeat from * all round, finish [5 chain 1sc] into each of next 7 spaces, 5 chain, slip stitch into 1st sc.

### Edging

3sc, 2 chain, slip stitch into 5th chain from hook (the picot) 3sc into space, * 1sc into each of next 3sc, 2sc into space, 1 picot 2sc into next space, 1sc into each of next 3sc, [3sc 1 picot 3sc] into each of next 9 spaces, repeat from * all round, join with slip stitch. Fasten off.

### TO FINISH

Weave any loose ends into the wrong side of the work. Lay the work out flat, then steam and press lightly.

# Organic Table Runner

Simply draw freehand a very amoeba-like shape onto a piece of graph paper, roughly the width and length you desire to fit your table or credenza. Work a collection of random motifs—some half motifs and some with extensions grafted on to make irregular shapes. Pin the finished motifs haphazardly onto your chosen shape and link them with chains. Then while they are still pinned onto the paper, add extra little bits to these linking chains to create a completely unique, one-off piece of creative crochet. This runner is made in mercerized cotton and is trimmed with jet beads— perfect for the modern coffee table or retro credenza.

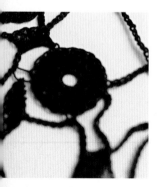  

# Making the Organic Table Runner

**SIZE**

Approx. 36 in. x 11 in. (92cm x 28cm), but size can be easily adjusted as required

**MATERIALS**

Graph paper and pencil

Approx. 1¾ oz. (50g) Yeoman Yarns Cotton Cannele or similar 4-ply mercerized cotton yarn (see page 170)

Hook size E/4

Approx. 12 ¼ in. (6mm) and 12 ⅛ in. (3mm) jet beads

Size #10 sharp needle and cotton thread

**GAUGE**

Working to an exact gauge is not essential (see Tip).

**TECHNIQUES USED**

Single, double, and half-double crochet, working in rounds, and free-form crochet.

For single crochet: see page 14

For double crochet: see page 16

For half-double crochet: see page 18

For working in rounds: see page 22

For free-form crochet: see page 24

**TIP**

**Gauge:** Don't worry about gauge too much! If your motifs ends up a bit bigger or smaller than the size given here, just add more motifs to achieve the required size.

**METHOD**

Sketch out the shape for your design onto graph paper to make a template. Make as many of the following as required for your design:

**Rosette A**

**Base ring:** Chain 7, join with slip stitch.

**Round 1:** Chain 1, 12sc into ring, join with slip stitch into 1st sc, 3 chain.

**Round 2:** 1dc into next stitch [3 chain, 1dc in each of next 2 stitches] 5 times, 3 chain, join with slip stitch to top of 3 chain.

**Rosette B**

**Base ring:** Chain 6, join with slip stitch.

**Round 1:** Chain 1, 16sc into ring, slip stitch to 1st sc.

**Round 2:** Chain 6, skip 2 stitches [1dc in next stitch, 3 chain, skip 1 stitch] 7 times, slip stitch to 3rd chain of 6 chain.

**Round 3:** Chain 1 [1sc, 1 half-double, 5dc, 1 half-double, 1sc in 3 chain space] 8 times, slip stitch to 1st sc.

### Rosette C
**Base ring:** Chain 10, join with slip stitch.
**Round 1:** 24sc into ring, slip stitch into 1st sc.
**Round 2:** [6 chain, skip 2sc, 1sc into next stitch] 8 times, slip stitch into 1st chain.
**Round 3:** [8sc into next 6 chain, space] 8 times, slip stitch into 1st sc.

### Rosette D
**Base ring:** Chain 10, join with slip stitch.
**Round 1:** 24 half-double crochet into ring, slip stitch into 1st sc.

### Rosette E
**Base ring:** Chain 6, join with slip stitch.
**Row 1:** Chain 1, 18sc into ring, 6 chain. Turn.
**Row 2:** Skip 2 stitches [1dc in next stitch, 3 chain, skip 1 stitch] 4 times. Turn.
**Row 3:** Chain 1 [1sc, 1 half-double, 5dc, 1 half-double, 1sc in 3 chain space] 4 times.

### TO FINISH
Pin each motif onto the paper template in the position required—in the sample photographed, the spaces between each motif are approx. 1½ in. (4cm). Onto the paper template, draw as many linking chains between the motifs as desired. Crochet the linking chains following the pencil lines, but keep the motifs attached to the template. Join to the first motif with a slip stitch, make a chain to the next motif, and join to that motif with a slip stitch. Insert a group of trebles at each intersection point of two or more chains. Weave in any yarn ends. Attach beads randomly as desired using sewing needle and cotton thread.

# Heirloom

These exquisite vintage-inspired pieces will give a special welcome to any new baby and can be treasured as keepsakes once baby has grown up. In a color palette of muted pastel shades and classic creams, this is a collection of adorable baby items ranging from blankets to a bonnet and bootees. Made in basic single and double crochet, these projects are embellished with small motifs and easy decorative edgings.

# Daisy-chain Crib Blanket

A beautiful project to make for a new baby's crib or stroller, this blanket is crocheted in wool cotton yarn, which feels wonderfully smooth and is very practical—it will keep baby snug in winter and comfortably cool during the warmer months. The crochet stitch used here imitates a woven fabric and creates an interesting texture. The tiny crocheted flowers and the picot-stitch trim pick out the colors of the vintage-style fabric backing the blanket. You could use patches of your favorite fabrics pieced together to make the backing even more individual.

# Making the Daisy-chain Crib Blanket

## SIZE

Approx. 50 in. x 35½ in. (127cm x 90cm)

## MATERIALS

Rowan Wool Cotton or a similar medium-weight cotton yarn (see page 170) in six colors:

**Color A:** 18 x 1¾ oz. (50g) balls in violet
**Color B:** 2 x 1¾ oz. (50g) balls in yellow
**Color C:** 1 x 1¾ oz. (50g) ball in camel
**Color D:** 1 x 1¾ oz. (50g) ball in russet
**Color E:** 1 x 1¾ oz. (50g) ball in green
**Color F:** 1 x 1¾ oz. (50g) ball in purple
Hook sizes F/5 and E/4

Approx. 52 in. x 37½ in. (132cm x 95cm) lightweight fabric, such as cotton, for backing
Tapestry needle
Size #10 sharp needle and sewing thread

## TECHNIQUES USED

Single and double crochet, and picot edging (see pattern)

For single crochet: see page 14

For double crochet: see page 16

## GAUGE

This blanket has a gauge of 22 stitches and 10 rows to 4 in. (10cm) measured over pattern of 1sc 1ch using a F/5 hook, or hook size required to achieve gauge.

## METHOD

**Foundation row:** Leaving a long, loose tail of yarn and using a hook size F/5, chain 184.

**Row 1:** Work 1sc into 4th chain from hook, * 1 chain, skip 1 chain, 1sc into next chain, repeat from * to end. Turn.

**Row 2:** Chain 2 to count as 1st sc and 1st 1 chain space, skip 1st sc and work 1sc into 1st 1 chain space, * chain 1, skip next sc, 1sc into next 1 chain space, repeat from * to end working last sc into chain space at edge. Turn.

Repeat Row 2 until work measures 45 in. (115cm) from foundation row edge. Fasten off.

### Picot edging

Work a simple picot-stitch edging all around the throw. Begin by joining a contrast yarn to a corner of the throw with a slip stitch, then work the edging as follows:

Using hook size E/4 and working 3sc into each corner, work 1 row sc around the

entire blanket, stitch for stitch and row for row. Join with slip stitch to 1st stitch.

Now work a triple-picot edging as follows: Chain 2, * 1dc in next 5sc, [chain 3, slip stitch into 3rd chain from hook] 3 times, slip stitch into top of last sc made. Repeat from * all the way around. In order to get a picot on each corner, you may have to adjust the number of sc between the picots at the end of a row. Fasten off.

Weave any loose ends into the work, using the tapestry needle.

### Flowers (make 24)

**Foundation chain:** Using hook size E/4 and contrast yarn, chain 2.
**Row 1:** 4sc into 2nd chain from hook,

slip stitch into 1st sc.
**Row 2:** Chain 3, work 3dc 3 chain and 1 slip stitch into same place as join, [1 slip stitch 3 chain 3dc 3 chain 1 slip stitch into next stitch) 3 times. [4 petals] Work 1 slip stitch in joining stitch, 8 chain, turn and starting with 2nd chain from hook, slip stitch back along chain toward the flower.

Fasten off, leaving a long tail of yarn, which can be used to attach flower to the blanket.

Make 24 or as many flowers as desired, in different contrasting colors.

### TO FINISH

Weave any loose ends into the work. Lay the work out flat. Steam and press

lightly. If necessary, pin out the work to keep the corners square.

Place the flowers all around the edges of the blanket, approx. 2 in. (5cm) in from the outer edge.

Pin and sew each flower into position very firmly using a tapestry needle and long tail of yarn, taking care to remove all pins.

Cut the fabric to size of the blanket, adding a hem allowance of 1 in. (2.5cm) all the way around. Pin and baste the fabric into position, turning under 1 in. (2.5cm) at each edge, smoothing the fabric and crocheted blanket as you go. Sew neatly with whipping stitches using the size #10 sharp needle and sewing thread to match the backing fabric. Remove all pins. Lightly steam and press once more.

# Soft Bear or Bunny

Perfect for the nursery, these little fellows sit and dangle their legs in a very relaxed manner. Both the bear and the bunny are made in glazed cotton yarn using basic single crochet. The head is worked in one piece to minimize assembly. The bottom and feet are stuffed with beanbag filling to provide weight and help the toys stay put. The faces are embroidered very simply using a contrasting colored cotton yarn, and there are two sets of ears to choose from to make either bear or bunny. (Bunny, of course, will require a pom-pom tail!)

# Making the Soft Bear or Bunny

Approx. 16 in. (40cm) long, measured from foot to top of ear

**MATERIALS**
3 x 1¾ oz. (50g) balls Rowan Cotton Glacé or similar medium-weight cotton yarn (see page 170)
Hook size C/2
½ yd. (½m) satin ribbon, ⅛ in. (3.0mm) wide
Polyester fiberfill
Poly pellets (available at craft stores)
Scraps of contrasting colored cotton yarn for embroidering eyes
Scraps of matching colored suede fabric for nose, ears, paws, and feet

**TECHNIQUES USED**
Single crochet and working in rounds

For single crochet: see page 14

For working in rounds: see page 22

**GAUGE**
This bear or bunny has a gauge of 20 stitches and 20 rows to 4 in. (10cm) measured over single crochet using a C/2 hook, or hook size required to achieve gauge.

**TIPS**
**Working in rounds:** When you work in rounds, you never have to turn the fabric. The right side is always facing you.
**Marking the beginning of a round:** Mark the beginning of each round to make it easier to keep your place.

**METHOD**
**Head (worked in one piece)**
**Foundation row:** Chain 17.
**Row 1:** 1sc in 2nd chain from hook, 1sc in every following chain, 1 chain. Turn. [16 stitches]
**Row 2:** 2sc in 1st sc, 5sc, 2sc in next sc, 2sc, 2sc in next sc, 5sc, 2sc in last sc, 1 chain. Turn. [20 stitches]
**Row 3:** 2sc in 1st sc, 7sc, 2sc in next sc, 2sc, 2sc in next sc, 7sc, 2sc in last sc, 1 chain. Turn. [24 stitches]
    Work 4 rows straight in sc.
**Next row:** 9sc, skip 1sc, 4sc, skip 1sc, sc to end, 1 chain. Turn.
**Next row:** 8sc, skip 1sc, 4sc, skip 1sc, sc to end, 1 chain. Turn. [20 stitches]
    Work 26 rows without shaping.

**Next row:** 1sc in 1st sc, skip 1sc, 6sc, skip 1sc, 2sc, skip 1sc, 6sc, skip 1sc, 1sc in last sc. [16 stitches]

Work 1 row straight in sc. Fasten off.

### Body (worked in one piece)

**Foundation row:** Chain 59.

**Row 1:** 1sc in 2nd chain from hook, 1sc in every chain to end, 1 chain. Turn. [58sc]

**Row 2:** Sc to end, 1 chain. Turn.

**Row 3:** 19sc, sc 2 together, 16sc, sc 2 together, 19sc, 1 chain. Turn. [56sc]

**Row 4:** Sc to end, 1 chain. Turn.

**Row 5:** 18sc, sc 2 together, 16sc, sc 2 together, 18sc. [54sc]

**Row 6:** Sc to end, 1 chain. Turn.

Continue decreasing as set at each end of alternate rows until 32sc remain.

Work 2 rows straight. Fasten off.

### Body base

**Foundation ring:** Chain 4, join with slip stitch to form ring.

**Round 1:** Chain 1, 8sc into ring, join with slip stitch to 1st sc.

**Round 2:** Chain 1, 2sc in each stitch to end, join with slip stitch. [16 stitches]

**Round 3:** Chain 1 [2sc in next stitch, 1sc], repeat to end, join with slip stitch. [24 stitches]

**Round 4:** Chain 1, [2sc, 2sc in next stitch] repeat to end, join with slip stitch. [32 stitches]

**Round 5:** Chain 1, [2sc in next stitch, 3sc] repeat to end, join with slip stitch. [40 stitches]

Continue increasing 8 stitches on every round until base measures 3¼ in. in diameter. Fasten off.

### Arms (make 2)

**Foundation ring:** Chain 12, join with slip stitch to form ring.

**Next round:** 1sc in each chain. [12 stitches]

Then work in rounds with 1sc in every sc until work measures 3¼ in. (8cm) long. (Use a colored thread to mark the end of each round.)

**Next round:** 2sc in next sc, 5sc, 2sc in next sc, 5sc. [14 stitches]

Work 5 more rounds without increasing.

**Next row:** Turn and work on 1st 7sc as follows: Chain 1, 7sc.

Now increase 1 stitch at each end of next and following 3rd row. [11 stitches]

Work 2 rows straight.

Decrease 1 stitch at each end of next and following 2 rows. Fasten off.

Rejoin yarn to remaining 7sc and work to match.

### Legs (make 2)

The foot is worked first, sewn, and the leg is worked last.

**Foundation row:** Chain 29.

**Row 1:** 1sc in 2nd chain from hook, 1sc in each chain to end. Turn each row with 1 chain. [28 stitches]

Increase 1 stitch at each end of next 2 rows. [32 stitches]

Work 1 row sc.

**Next row:** Sc 2 together, sc to last 2 stitches, sc 2 together.

Repeat last row 5 times more. [20 stitches] Fasten off.

Fold foot in half. Sew sole of foot, round toe, and the first 2sc either side of top. Rejoin yarn to top of foot and working in rounds [18 stitches] sc from top of foot until leg measures 4¼ in. (11cm) long.

Fasten off.

### Bear ears (make 2)

**Foundation row:** Chain 7.

**Row 1:** 2sc in 2nd chain from hook, sc to last chain, 2sc in last chain.

Turn each row with 1 chain.

**Next row:** 2sc in 1st stitch, sc to last stitch, 2sc in last stitch.

Work 1 row sc.

**Next row:** 2sc in 1st stitch, sc to last stitch, 2sc in last stitch.

Work 2 rows sc.

**Next row:** Sc 2 together, sc to last 2 stitches, sc 2 together.

Work 1 row sc.

Repeat last 2 rows once more. Fasten off.

### Bunny ears (make 2)

**Foundation row:** Chain 9.

**Row 1:** 1sc into 2nd chain from hook, 1sc in each chain to end. [8 stitches] Turning each row with 1 chain, work 3 rows sc.

**Next row:** 2sc into 1st stitch, sc to last stitch, 2sc in last stitch.

Work 11 rows sc.

**Next row:** Sc 2 together, sc to last 2 stitches, sc 2 together.

Work 1 row sc.

Repeat last 2 rows until 4 stitches remain. Fasten off.

### Bunny tail

Cut out two circles of cardboard, approx. 1¼ in. (3cm) in diameter and cut identical ½-in. (1.5-cm) holes in the center of each. Hold the two circles together and wind the yarn around the cardboard circles. Work as many layers as you can before the center hole disappears.

Using sharp scissors, slip one of the blades between the two outer layers of

cardboard and cut around the circumference of the circle. Slip a length of yarn between the two layers around the center of what will become the pom-pom, pull tight, and knot the yarn.

Cut away the cardboard, shake, fluff up the pom-pom, and trim to shape.

Attach the pom-pom to the bottom of the bunny.

### TO FINISH

For the head, fold in half and join the side seams. Stuff firmly with the polyester fiberfill.

For the arms, join the seam around each hand and stuff firmly with the stuffing.

For the legs, pour poly pellets into each foot and then stuff firmly with the fiberfill.

For the body, fold in half and join the seam down the center back.

Attach the head to body at the neck. Pour poly pellets into the base of the body and stuff the remaining body with the fiberfill.

Attach the base to the body.

Sew the legs and arms in position on the body as shown on page 115.

Attach the ears to the head. Embroider the eyes using contrasting colored yarn as shown. Cut out and sew in place a small triangle of suede fabric for the nose. Cut out and sew in place small patches of suede fabric for the ears, paws, and feet.

Wrap a short length of satin ribbon around the bear's or bunny's neck and tie into a neat bow.

# Baby's First Cardigan

The quintessential baby cardigan never goes out of fashion, as it is perfect for special occasions, such as a christening or first outing. This is a good basic cardigan pattern that can be embellished to suit your own taste. Here it is edged in shiny satin ribbon that contrasts beautifully with the matte-finish glazed cotton yarn. It is decorated with flowers crocheted in the same yarn and finished with pretty mother-of-pearl buttons, but it could just as easily be trimmed with ribbon bows or rosebuds.

# Making the Baby's First Cardigan

## SIZES

| To fit age (months): | 0–3 | 3–6 | 6–9 |
|---|---|---|---|
| Baby's chest: | 16 in. | 17 in. | 18 in. |
| | 41cm | 43.5cm | 46cm |
| Actual chest: | 20 in. | 22 in. | 24 in. |
| | 50cm | 55cm | 60cm |
| Length: | 9½ in. | 11½ in. | 13½ in. |
| | 24.5cm | 29.5cm | 34.5cm |
| Sleeve length: | 5¾ in. | 7¼ in. | 8 in. |
| | 15cm | 19cm | 21cm |

## MATERIALS

4 (5: 5) x 1¾ oz. balls Rowan Cotton Glacé or similar 4-ply cotton yarn (see page 170)
Hook sizes C/2 and D/3 or hook sizes required to achieve gauge
Approx. 12 (14: 15) yd. (12: 14: 15m) satin ribbon, ⅛ in. (3.0mm) wide

5 small buttons, ½ in. (1.5cm) in diameter
Tapestry needle

## TECHNIQUES USED

Double crochet, simple shaping, and picot edging (see pattern)

For double crochet: see page 16

## GAUGE

This cardigan has a gauge of 20dc and 11 rows to 4 in. (10cm) measured over double crochet using a D/3 hook, or hook size required to achieve gauge.

## TIP

**Gauge:** Make a sample swatch of crochet to test your stitch size. If you are getting more than 20dc to 4 in. (10cm), try a larger hook size; less the 20dc to 4 in. (10cm), a smaller hook size. Don't worry too much about the number of rows to 4 in. (10cm) as you can easily adjust the length.

## METHOD

### Back

**Foundation chain:** Using a hook size D/3, chain 53 (58: 63).

**Foundation row:** Work 1dc in 4th chain from hook then 1dc in each chain to end. Turn. [50 (55: 60) stitches]

**Row 1:** Chain 3 to count as 1st dc, 1dc into each dc to end. Turn.

Repeat row 1 until work measures 5 (6¼: 7½) in. (13: 16.5: 19.5cm). Turn. Do not work 3 chain.

**Shape armhole:** Slip stitch over 1st

5 stitches of next row, 3 chain, 1dc in each dc to the last 5 stitches. Turn. [40 (45: 50) stitches]

Continue working in dc without shaping until armhole measures 4¼ (5½: 5¾) in. (11.5: 13: 15cm).

**Shape shoulders and back neck:** Work dc across 1st 12 (14: 15) dc, then sc across next 16 (17: 20) dc, 3 chain, then work 1dc across remaining 12 (14: 15) dc. Fasten off.

### Left Front
**Foundation chain:** Chain 28 (31: 33).
**Foundation row:** As foundation row given for Back. [25 (28: 30) chain stitches]
**Row 1:** As Row 1 given for Back.
Repeat Row 1 until work matches Back to armhole shaping.
**Shape armhole:** Slip stitch across 1st 5 stitches, 3 chain, dc to end. Turn. [20 (23: 25) stitches]

Continue working in dc without shaping until armhole measures 3 (3½: 4⅜) in. (7.5: 9: 11cm) finishing at armhole edge.
**Shape neck:** Dc to last 5 stitches. Turn. [15 (18: 20) stitches]

Decrease 1 stitch at neck edge of next 3 (4: 5) rows. [12 (14: 15) stitches]

Work to match Back to shoulder. Fasten off.

### Right Front
Work to match Left Front, reversing shaping.

### Sleeves (make 2)
**Foundation chain:** Chain 35 (39: 41).
**Foundation row:** As foundation row given for Back. [32 (36: 38) stitches]

Work 3 rows dc.

Now increase 1 stitch at each end of next and every alternate row until 46 (52: 58) dc.

Continue without shaping until work measures 5¾ (7¼: 8) in. (15: 19: 21cm) from start.

Mark both ends of last row.

Work 2 more rows of dc. Fasten off.

### TO FINISH
Weave any loose ends into the work.

Lay work out flat. Steam and press lightly.

Sew the shoulder seams. Sew the sleeve seams. The 2 last rows are stitched along the armhole shaping.

Sew side and sleeve seams.

### Edging
Using hook size C/2 and satin ribbon, with right side of work facing and starting at center back neck, work edging as follows: * 1 slip stitch into 1st stitch, 3 chain, 1 slip stitch into same stitch, 1 slip stitch into each of next 3 stitches, repeat from * all round edge of jacket.

Fasten off. Weave in any ribbon ends.

### Flowers (make 4–6)
**Foundation chain:** Using hook size D/3, chain 2.
**Row 1:** 4sc into 2nd chain from hook, slip stitch into 1st sc.
**Row 2:** 3 chain 3 dc 3 chain 1 slip stitch into same place as join, 1 slip stitch 3 chain 3 dc 3 chain 1 slip stitch into next 3sc. [4 petals]

Work 1 slip stitch in joining stitch, 8 chain, turn, starting with 2nd chain from hook slip stitch back along chain toward flower.

Fasten off, leaving a long yarn end to use to attach the flower.

Sew on the buttons and sew the flowers onto both fronts.

# Baby's First Bonnet

The perfect accessory to complement the cardigan, this little bonnet has timeless appeal. It is worked in a combination of all the basic stitches with a contrast-stitch trim. The bonnet edge is threaded with fine satin ribbon and finished with wide satin-sash bows. Although classic in cream, this bonnet would also be oh-so-cute in other colors. Make the bonnet as part of a set, along with a matching pair of Baby's First Bootees (see page 130)—a gift that will delight any new parents.

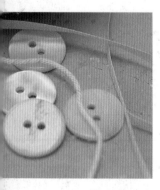

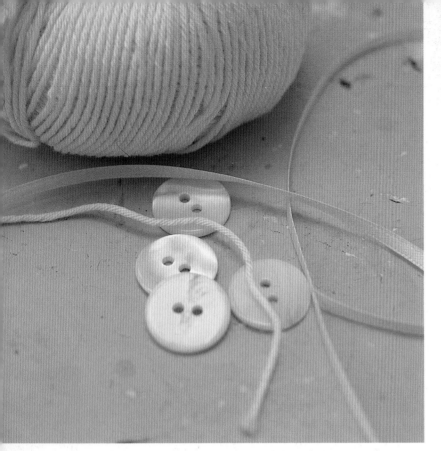

# Making the Baby's First Bonnet

### SIZE

One size—approx. 5 in. (12.5cm) from center of crown to brim—to fit 0–3 months

### MATERIALS

2 x 1¾ oz. (50g) balls Rowan Cotton Glacé or a similar sport-weight cotton yarn (see page 170)
Hook size D/3 or hook size required to achieve gauge
Approx. ½ yd. (0.5m) fine satin ribbon, ⅛ in. (3mm) wide
Approx. 1½ yd. (1.5m) wide satin ribbon, 1 in. (2.5cm) wide
Tapestry needle

### TECHNIQUES USED

Single, double, half-double, and treble crochet and simple shaping and edging (see pattern)

For single crochet: see page 14
For double crochet: see page 16
For half-double crochet: see page 18
For treble crochet: see page 19

### GAUGE

This bonnet has a gauge of 8 stitches and 8 rows to 2 in. (5cm) measured over the two row pattern.

### METHOD

**Foundation row:** Leaving a long, loose tail of yarn, chain 5.
**Row 1:** 2sc in 2nd chain from hook, [2sc in next chain] repeat to end. Turn. [8 stitches]
**Row 2:** Chain 2, [2dc in sc] repeat to last stitch, 1dc in last stitch. Turn. [15 stitches]
**Row 3 and every alternate row:** [1 chain, 1sc in next stitch], repeat to end. Turn.
**Row 4:** Chain 3, [2dc in sc] repeat to end. Turn. [30 stitches]
**Row 6:** Chain 3, [2dc in next stitch, 1dc] repeat to end. Turn. [45 stitches]
**Row 8:** Chain 3, dc to end. Turn.
**Row 10:** Chain 3, 2dc, 2dc in next stitch, [3dc, 2dc in next stitch] repeat to last 2 stitches, 2dc. Turn. [56 stitches]
**Row 12:** As Row 8.
**Row 14:** Chain 3, 4dc, [2dc in next stitch, 5dc] repeat to last 4 stitches, 2dc in next stitch, 3dc. Turn. [65 stitches]
**Row 15:** [chain 1, 1dc in next stitch] repeat

to end. Turn.

**Row 16:** Chain 3, dc to end. Turn.

Repeat Rows 15 and 16 until work measures 5½ in. (14cm), finishing at the end of a Row 15.

**Reverse work as follows:**

**Next row:** [Chain 1, dc to end. Turn.]

**Next row:** As Row 16.

**Next row:** As Row 15.

Repeat last two rows.

**Next row:** Chain 2, 2 half-double, 2 half-double in next stitch, [3 half-double, 2 half-double in next stitch] 15 times, 2 half-double. Turn. [82 stitches.]

**Next row:** As Row 15.

**Next row:** Chain 3, 3tr in next stitch, [skip 3sc, 3sc, skip 3sc, 7tr in next stitch] repeat to last 10sc, skip 3sc, 3sc, skip 3sc, 4tr in last stitch. Turn.

**Next row:** Chain 1, sc to end. Fasten off.

## TO FINISH

Weave any loose ends into the work.

Lay the work out flat. Steam and press lightly.

Join the seam from the center of the crown to the end of the shapings.

Turn back the trim. Thread the fine ribbon through the eyelet holes at the very edges of the trim.

Cut the wider ribbon in half crosswise. Make a big bow at one end of each piece and attach one to each side of the bonnet as shown.

# Baby's First Bootees

There is nothing quite like a pair of tiny bootees with sweet rosebuds to prompt you to take up a

hook and learn to crochet. Reminiscent of little dancing shoes, these rosebud bootees are irresistible.

Made in glazed cotton and worked in single crochet with simple increases and decreases, they are

finished with butter-soft suede soles, satin ribbon ties, and dainty crocheted flowers. They are a

delight both to make and give.

# Making the Baby's First Bootees

## SIZES

To fit age (months):  0–3   3–6   6–9
Length:               3⅛ in. 3½ in. 4 in.
                      8cm    9cm    10cm

## MATERIALS

1 x 1¾ oz. (50g) ball Rowan Cotton Glacé or similar sport-weight cotton yarn (see page 170)

Hook size D/3 or hook size required to achieve gauge

1¼ yd. (1.25m) satin ribbon, ¼ in. (1cm) wide

Tapestry needle

Size #10 sharp needle and cotton thread

Scraps of suede fabric for soles

## TECHNIQUES USED

Single crochet and working in rounds

For single crochet: see page 14

For working in rounds: see page 22

## GAUGE

These bootees have a gauge of 6 stitches and 6 rows to 1 in. (2.5cm) measured over single crochet using a D/3 hook, or hook size required to achieve gauge.

## TIP

The bootees are made in one piece, starting with the sole. Make sure to secure all motifs very carefully. Take time and care in checking for any remaining pins once the bootees are sewn together.

## METHOD

### Sole

**Foundation row:** Leaving a long, loose tail of yarn, chain 8.

**Row 1:** 1sc into 2nd chain from hook, sc to end. Turn.

**Row 2:** Chain 1, 2sc into next sc, sc to last sc, 2sc into last sc. Turn.

**Row 3:** Chain 1, sc to end. Turn.

Repeat Row 3 until work measures 3⅛ (3¼: 4) in. (8: 9: 10cm) from start.

**Next row:** Chain 1, skip 1sc, sc to last 2sc, skip 1sc, 1sc in last sc, turn.

### Upper

**Round 1:** Chain 1, 7 (7: 7)sc, 14 (16: 18)sc along side of sole, 7 (7: 7)sc along toe, 14 (16: 18)sc along other side of sole and join with a slip stitch into 1ch at beg of round. [42 (46: 50) stitches]

**Round 2:** Chain 1, sc to end, join with a slip stitch into 1st ch.

Repeat Round 2 twice.

**Round 5:** Chain 1, 20 (22: 24)sc, skip 1sc, 7 (7: 7)sc, skip 1sc, 13 (15: 17)sc, join with slip stitch into 1st chain. [42 (46: 50) stitches]

**Round 6:** Chain 1, 20 (22: 24)sc, skip 1sc, 5 (5: 5)sc, skip 1sc, 13 (15: 17)sc, join with slip stitch into 1st chain. [40 (44: 48) stitches]

**Round 7:** Chain 1, 20 (22: 24)sc, skip 1sc, 3 (3: 3)sc, skip 1sc, 13 (15: 17)sc, join with slip stitch into 1st chain. [38 (42: 46) stitches]

**Round 8:** Chain 1, 20 (22: 24)sc, skip 1sc, 1sc, skip 1sc, 13 (15: 17)sc, join with slip stitch into 1st chain. [36 (38: 44) stitches]

**Round 9:** Chain 1, 5sc, 5 chain slip stitch into same stitch to make a loop at the heel for the ribbon, 11 (13: 15)sc, [skip 1sc, 1sc into next sc] 5 times, sc to end, join with slip stitch into 1st chain. Fasten off.

**To make rosebud (make 2)**

**Foundation chain:** Chain 2.

**Row 1:** 5sc into 2nd chain from hook, slip stitch into 1st sc.

**Row 2:** Chain 3, 3dc 3ch 1 slip stitch into same place as join, * 1 slip stitch in next sc, 3 chain 3dc 3 chain 1 slip stitch in same sc, repeat from * 3 times. [5 petals] Fasten off.

**TO FINISH**

Attach a rosebud to front of each bootee using yarn and a tapestry needle. Cut length of ribbon in half crosswise and thread through the loop and knot securely. Using sole as a template, trace its outline onto the suede. Cut out 2 pieces. Sew onto bottom of each bootee with small, neat whipping stitches using cotton thread and a size #10 sharp needle.

# Cuddly Blanket

Every new baby deserves the best. Crocheted in the softest, most beautiful hand-dyed alpaca yarn, this blanket is pure luxury. The sheer simplicity of the design complements the ultimate softness of the wool and creates an heirloom piece that even beginning crocheters will be able to make and give with pride. The blanket is made in one piece, then trimmed separately with a very simple lace edging, so it is very easy to make as small or as large as you wish. It is perfect for a carry shawl, for the crib, or for the stroller.

# Making the Cuddly Blanket

**SIZE**

Approx. 30 in. x 30 in. (75cm x 75cm)

**MATERIALS**

8 x 3¾ oz. (100g) skeins Blue Skies Chunky Alpaca or a similar worsted-weight wool yarn (see page 170)

Hook sizes I/9 and J/10 or hook sizes required to achieve gauge

**TECHNIQUES USED**

Single, double, half-double, treble, and triple treble crochet, and working in rounds

For single crochet: see page 14

For double crochet: see page 16

For half-double crochet: see page 18

For treble crochet: see page 19

For triple treble crochet: see page 20

For working in rounds: see page 22

**GAUGE**

This blanket has a gauge of 11 stitches to 4 in. (10cm) and 4 rows to 3 in. (7.5cm) measured over double crochet with a J/10 hook, or hook size required to achieve gauge.

**TIP**

**Working in rounds:** When you work in rounds, you never have to turn the fabric. The right side is always facing you.

**METHOD**

**Foundation ring:** Leaving a long, loose tail of yarn and using a hook size J/10, chain 6 and join length of chain into ring by working a slip stitch into 1st chain made.

**Round 1:** Chain 5 (counts as 1dc and 2 chain), [3dc into ring, 2 chain] 3 times, 2dc into ring, slip stitch to 3rd of 5 chain. [4 groups of 3 doubles]

**Round 2:** Slip stitch into corner arch, chain 7 (counts as 1dc and 4 chain), * 2dc into same arch, 1dc into each dc across side of square **, 2dc into next arch, 4 chain, repeat from * twice and from * to ** again, 1dc into same arch as 7 chain, slip stitch to 3rd of 7 chain. [4 groups of 7 doubles]

**Round 3:** As Round 2. [4 groups of 11 doubles]

**Round 4:** As Round 2. [4 groups of 15 doubles]

Continue increasing in the same way until 19 rounds have been completed, which will be 4 groups of 75 doubles.

Do not fasten off but continue with border as follows:

## Border

Using a hook size I/9, chain 1, 1sc into same place as 1 chain [chain 6, 1sc in 2nd chain from hook, 1 half-double in next chain, 1dc in next chain, 1tr in next chain, 1 double treble in next chain, skip 4 stitches, 1sc in next stitch] repeat all round.

Make sure that the triangles sit neatly on the corners by working the sc at the start and end of the triangle within the arch.

Fasten off.

## TO FINISH

Weave any loose ends into the work.
Lay work out flat. Steam and press lightly.

# Vintage

In this section I have chosen the ultimate in crochet: a collection of personal accessories to create a fashionable vintage look. Dress up in a cascading ruffled scarf, fasten a flower pin to your lapel, or style a delicate free-form crochet camisole with your favorite worn denims. The projects vary from the very simple trio of ribbon bracelets, which can all be made in less than an hour, to the more complex camisole, which requires a greater degree of skill and the confidence to experiment.

# Ruffled Scarf

Add a touch of vintage elegance to any outfit with this cascading ruffled scarf. Worked in long rounds, it is an extremely quick project to make. Start crocheting it today, and you will be wearing the scarf by this evening! I can guarantee that everyone else will want one, too, so you will surely be making this scarf pattern time after time—experiment with lots of textures and colors, even in the same scarf, to create something completely individual.

# Making the Ruffled Scarf

**SIZE**

Approx. 57 in. (145cm) long

**MATERIALS**

3 x 3¾ oz. (100g) balls Rowan Biggy Print or
similar chunky wool yarn (see page 170) OR
3 x 1¾ oz. (50g) balls Rowan R2 Paper Yarn
or similar paper yarn (see page 170)
Hook size L/11 for wool yarn OR
hook size J/10 for paper yarn, or hook sizes
required to achieve gauge
Tapestry needle

**TECHNIQUES USED**

Single crochet and double crochet

For single crochet: see page 14

For double crochet: see page 16

**GAUGE**

Two-pattern repeats to 3½ in. (9cm),
when measured along the starting chain.
Depth of pattern is 3½ in. (9cm) when
measured from starting chain to edge of
central picot loop.

**TIP**

**Gauge:** Don't worry about gauge too
much! Because this scarf does not have to
be an exact size, you can add stitches until
it is the length required.

**METHOD**

**Foundation chain:** Working loosely and
using hook size L/11 with wool yarn and
hook size J/10 with paper yarn, chain 117.

**Row 1:** Work 1sc into 3rd chain from hook,
then 1sc into each chain to end. Turn.

**Row 2:** 5 chain, skip 1st 4sc, slip stitch into
next sc [5 chain, skip 3sc, slip stitch into
next sc] repeat to end. Turn. [29 spaces]

**Row 3:** 1 chain to count as 1st sc, 7sc into
1st 5 chain space, 8sc into each 5 chain
space to end.

Repeat Rows 2 and 3 along opposite
side of foundation chain. Turn.

**Round 4:** 4 chain to count as 1st dc and
1 chain [1dc, 1 chain into next sc] repeat
round both sides. Join with slip stitch to
3rd of 4 chain.

**For the paper scarf only**

**Round 5:** [5 chain, skip next space, sc in
next space] repeat to end of round. Join
with slip stitch to base of 1st loop.

**Round 6:** Slip stitch across 1st 3 chain of

1st loop, [6 chain, 1sc in next loop] repeat to end of round. Join with slip stitch to base of 1st loop.

**Round 7 (picot edge):** Slip stitch across 1st 3 chain of 1st loop, [6 chain, 1sc in 3rd chain from hook, 3 chain, 1 sc into next loop] repeat to end, slip stitch to base of 1st loop.

Weave any yarn ends into the work using a tapestry needle.

# Heart-shaped Pillow

The beauty of crochet is its versatility; it can be made in small, easy pieces that may then be assembled in different ways. This pretty heart-shaped pillow is worked in this manner. Simple textured stitches are created with very basic shaping and pieced together like a puzzle. They are joined with chains to create large spaces through which the rich satin lining is glimpsed and then further embellished with self-color floral motifs. It is finished with a very easy edging to emphasize the heart shape.

# Making the Heart-shaped Pillow

## PILLOW SIZE
Approx. 18 in. x 15 in. (48cm x 38cm) at widest point

## MATERIALS
Approx. 10 oz. (250g) Yeomans Cotton Cannele or similar 4-ply mercerized cotton yarn (see page 170)
Hook sizes B/1, C/2, D/3, and E/4 or hook sizes required to achieve gauge
Graph paper, one square to 1 in. (2.5cm)
Tapestry needle
Pillow form

## GAUGE
This pillow has a gauge of 12 stitches and 5 rows to 2 in. (5cm) measured over doubles, using a D/3 hook, or hook size required to achieve gauge.

## TECHNIQUES USED
This cushion is made up of various different shapes of crochet using a variety of stitches.
For basic crochet stitches: see pages 14–22

## TIP
Before starting work, take time to draw the heart shape onto graph paper. Mark each shape onto your drawing and crochet to fit these shapes. Pin each piece right side up to the paper as you go.

## METHOD
### Rose bower square for Front
**Base ring:** With D/3 hook, chain 6 and join into a ring with a slip stitch.
**Round 1:** Chain 5, [1dc into ring, chain 2] 7 times, slip stitch into 3rd of 5 chain. [8 spaces]

**Round 2:** Into each space, work [1sc, 1 half-double, 3dc, 1 half-double and 1sc], slip stitch into 1st sc. [8 petals]
**Round 3:** 1sc into same place as slip stitch, [4 chain, 1sc between next 2 petals], repeat to end, slip stitch into 1st sc.
**Round 4:** Into each loop work [1sc, 1 half-double, 5dc, 1 half-double and 1sc], slip stitch into 1st sc.
**Round 5:** As Round 3.
**Round 6:** Into each loop work [1sc, 1 half-double, 7dc, 1 half-double and 1sc], slip stitch into 1st sc.
**Round 7:** As Round 3.
**Round 8:** Into each loop work [1sc, 1 half-double, 1dc, 7tr, 1dc, 1 half-double and 1sc], slip stitch into 1st sc.
**Round 9:** Slip stitch to center treble of 1st petal, 1sc in same place as last slip stitch, * chain 7, leaving last loop of each treble on hook work 3 treble into center treble of next petal, yarn over hook and pull through all loops on hook [cluster made], chain 4, into same treble work [3 treble cluster, chain 4 and a 3 treble cluster], chain 7, 1sc into center treble of next petal, repeat from * all round, slip stitch into 1st sc.
**Round 10:** Slip stitch to center 3 treble cluster of 1st 3 treble cluster group, chain 3, 2dc into same stitch * chain 1, 3dc into next space, [chain 1, into next space work 3dc 1 chain and 3dc] twice, chain 1, 3dc into next space, chain 1, into tip of next cluster work 3dc 3 chain and 3dc, repeat from * all round, omitting 3dc 3 chain and 3dc at end of last repeat, 3dc into same place as 1st 2dc, chain 1, 1dc into 3rd of 3 chain.
**Rounds 11–13:** Chain 3, 2dc into space just

formed, * [1 chain, 3dc into next space] 7 times, chain 1, into corner space work 3dc 3 chain and 3dc, repeat from * all round, omitting 3dc 3 chain and 3dc at end of last repeat, 3dc into same place as 1st 2dc, chain 1, 1dc into 3rd of 3 chain.
**Round 14:** As Round 11, omitting 3dc 3 chain and 3dc at end of last repeat; 3dc into same place as 1st 2dc, chain 3, slip stitch to 3rd of 3 chain. Fasten off, leaving long end.

### Plain motif for Back
**Base ring:** Using D/3 hook, chain 6 and join into a ring with a slip stitch.
**Round 1:** Chain 5 [count as 1dc and 2 chain], [3dc into ring, chain 2] 3 times, 2dc into ring, slip stitch to 3rd of 5 chain. [4 groups of 3dc]
**Round 2:** Slip stitch into corner arch, chain 7 [count as 1dc and 4 chain], * 2dc into same arch, 1dc into each dc across side of square **, 2dc into next arch, chain 4, repeat from * twice and from * to ** again, 1dc into same arch as 7 chain, slip stitch to 3rd of 7 chain. [4 groups of 7dc]
**Round 3:** As Round 2. [4 groups of 11dc]
**Round 4:** As Round 2. [4 groups of 15dc]
　　Continue increasing in the same way until 11 rounds have been completed, which will be 4 groups of 43dc.

### Crossed double sections for Front and Back (make 2)
**Two crossed doubles:** Skip next stitch, 1dc into next stitch, 1dc into skipped stitch working over previous dc.
**Foundation row:** Using D/3 hook, chain 36.
**Row 1:** Skip 3 chain [count as 1dc], * 2 crossed dc over next 2 chain; repeat from *

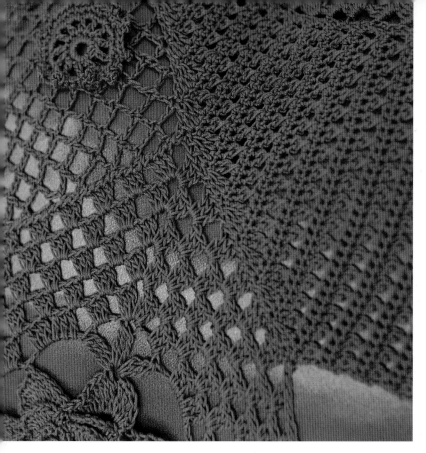

ending 1dc into last chain. Turn.

**Row 2:** Chain 1 [count as 1sc], skip 1 stitch, 1sc into next and each stitch to end, working last stitch into top of turning chain.

**Row 3:** Chain 3 [count as 1dc], skip 1 stitch, * work 2 crossed dc over next 2 stitches, repeat from * ending 1dc into turning chain. Turn.

Repeat Rows 2 and 3 until work measures 4⅜ in. (11cm), ending with a Row 2.

Shape top by working 3dc together at the end of every crossed dc row [i.e., decreasing 2 stitches at the end of row], and decrease 1 stitch at the beginning of every sc row by working 2sc together. Continue decreasing like this until 1 stitch left. Fasten off, leaving long yarn end for sewing.

### Filet sections for Front and Back (make 2)

**Foundation chain:** Using C/2 hook, chain 44.

**Row 1:** 1dc in 8th chain from hook, [chain 2, skip 2 stitches of base chain and work 1dc in next chain] repeat to end. [13 squares in total]

**Row 2:** Chain 5, [1dc into the dc below, chain 2], repeat to end of row working 1dc into 3rd chain stitch of previous row.

Repeat Row 2 until work measures 5 in. (12.5cm). Shape top by decreasing 1 block at each end of every row until 1 block remains. Fasten off, leaving a tail end for sewing.

### Heart Tops (make 4)

**Foundation chain:** Using C/2 hook, chain 12, slip stitch to 1st chain to form circle.

**Row 1:** Chain 5 [1t into circle, 1 chain] 5 times, 1tr into circle. Turn.

**Row 2:** Chain 5, * leaving last loop of each stitch on hook work 4dc into next 1 chain space, yarn over and draw through all 5

loops on hook (cluster made), chain 2, repeat from * into each space all round, ending with cluster into space formed by turning chain, chain 2, 1dc into 3rd turning chain. Turn.

**Row 3:** Chain 5, 4dc into 1st 2 chain space, * [3 chain, 1sc into next 2 chain space] twice, chain 3 *, [4dc, chain 2, 4dc] into next 2 chain space, repeat from * to * once more, 4dc into space formed by turning chain, chain 2, 1dc into 3rd turning chain. Turn.

**Row 4:** Chain 5, 4dc into 1st 2 chain space, chain 1, skip 1st 3 chain space, * [4dc into next 3 chain space, chain 1] twice *, [4dc, chain 2, 4dc] into next 2 chain space, chain 1, repeat from * to * once more, 4dc into space formed by turning chain, chain 2, 1dc into 3rd turning chain. Turn.

**Row 5:** Chain 4, * 4dc into 1st 2 chain space, * [4dc into next 1 chain space] 3 times *, [4dc, 2 chain, 4dc] into next 2

chain space, repeat from * to * once more, 4dc into space formed by turning chain, chain 1, 1dc into 3rd turning chain. Turn.

Continue until triangle is required size. Fasten off, leaving a tail end for sewing.

## TO FINISH

Pin pieces to heart-shaped graph paper drawing and sew together while still pinned to the paper. This helps to keep the heart shape intact.

Using C/2 hook work around the edge as follows: starting at the bottom tip of the heart, 36sc along edge of square motif, chain 28 across gap, 31sc along crossed double section, 124sc across top of heart, 31sc along filet section, chain 28 across gap and 36sc along second edge of square motif. Work another row sc, working 1sc into every sc and 1sc into each chain across gaps.

With wrong sides together, oversew the two pieces halfway around, insert pillow form, and finish sewing the gap.

Fill in gaps with the following motifs:

### Magic circles (make 2)
**Base ring:** With C/2 hook, chain 16 and join into a ring with a slip stitch.
**Round 1:** Chain 2 [count as 1 half-double], work 35 half-double into ring, join with slip stitch to 2nd of 2 chain at beginning of round.
**Round 2:** Chain 1, work 1sc into same stitch as last slip stitch [chain 5, skip 2 half-double, 1sc into next half-double] 11 times, chain 5, slip stitch into 1st sc.

Fasten off, leaving a tail end for sewing.

### Lace triangle (make 2)
**Base ring:** Wind yarn 7 times round little finger to form a ring.

**Round 1:** Using C/2 hook, chain 1, 12sc into ring, slip stitch to 1st sc.
**Round 2:** Chain 10 [count as 1dc and 7 chain arch], skip 1st 2sc, * 1dc into next sc, chain 3, skip 1sc, 1dc into next sc, chain 7, skip 1sc, repeat from * once, dc into next sc, chain 3, skip last sc, slip stitch to 3rd of 10 chain.
**Round 3:** Chain 3 [count as 1dc], into next chain arch work [3dc, chain 7, 4dc], * 3dc into next chain arch, [4dc, chain 7, 4dc] into next chain arch, repeat from * once, 3dc into last chain arch, slip stitch to top of 3 chain.

Fasten off, leaving a tail end for sewing.

### Lace edging
**Foundation chain:** Using B/1 hook, chain 6.
**Row 1:** 1dc into 4th chain from hook and into next of next 2 chain leaving last loop of each on hook, yarn over and draw through all loops on hook [cluster made], chain 5, 1dc into single loop of 5th chain from hook, [chain 2, 1dc into same place] 4 times, 1 double treble into same place as last dc of cluster was made, chain 7. Turn.
**Row 2:** Skip 1st dc, 1sc into next dc, chain 3. Turn.
**Row 3:** 1dc into each of 1st 3 of 7 turning chain leaving last loop of each on hook and complete a cluster as before, chain 5, 1dc into single loop of 5th chain from hook, [chain 2, 1dc in same place] 4 times, 1 double treble into same place as last treble of cluster was made, chain 7. Turn.

Repeat Rows 2 and 3 until lace fits around the outside edge of the pillow.

### TO FINISH
Pin the lace edging all around the outside edge of the pillow and hand sew into position, accentuating its heart shape.

Weave in any yarn ends. Crochet as

many of the following motifs as preferred and attach to front of cushion:

### Wheel motif
**Base ring:** With C/2 hook, chain 6 and join into a ring with a slip stitch.
**Round 1:** Chain 1, 12sc into ring, slip stitch to 1st sc.
**Round 2:** Chain 4, * 1dc, 1 chain, repeat from * to end, slip stitch to 3rd of 4 chain.
**Round 3:** Chain 1, * 3sc in next chain space, repeat from * to end, slip stitch to 1st sc.
**Round 4:** * Chain 4, slip stitch to 1st chain to make picot, 3sc, repeat from * to end, slip stitch to base of 1st picot. Fasten off.

### Trefoil motif
**Round 1:** With C/2 hook, chain 16, slip stitch into 1st chain (1st loop formed), [chain 15, slip stitch into same chain as last slip stitch] twice.
**Round 2:** Chain 1, * 28sc into next loop, slip stitch into same chain as slip stitches of Round 1, repeat from * twice.
**Round 3:** Slip stitch into each of 1st 3sc, chain 1, 1sc into same stitch as last slip stitch, 23sc, * skip 4sc, 24sc, repeat from * once.

Fasten off, leaving a tail end for sewing.

### Flower motif
**Foundation row:** Using E/4 hook, chain 2.
**Row 1:** 4sc into 2nd chain from hook, slip stitch into 1st sc.
**Row 2:** Chain 3, 3dc 3 chain 1 slip stitch into same place as join, * 1 slip stitch, 3 chain 3dc 3 chain 1 slip stitch in next sc, repeat from * 3 times. [4 petals]

Work 1 slip stitch in joining stitch, 8 chain, turn, starting with 2nd chain from hook slip stitch back along chain towards flower.

Fasten off, leaving a tail end for sewing.

# Flower Pin

Currently, this is an extremely popular accessory, taking its inspiration from vintage apparel. It can be made in a variety of yarns, colors, and textures, with various decorative embellishments. It is a perfect small project to personalize an outfit and makes an ideal gift for a cherished friend. Make this project time and time again in seasonal tweeds with a sparkly sequin trim or in more delicate organza, satin, and shiny cotton to add a little girly glamour to a sundress or jacket.

# Making the Flower Pin

## SIZE
Approx. 2¾ in. (7cm) in diameter without leaves. Make the flowers larger or smaller by using a larger or smaller hook.

## MATERIALS
Small amount of Yeoman's Cotton Cannele or similar sport-weight mercerized cotton yarn (see page 170)
Hook size 8
Scraps of fabric, such as tweed or wool, for leaves
Scraps of felt, for backing
Sequins
Size #10 sharp needle and cotton sewing thread in matching color to yarn
Rustproof safety pins

## TECHNIQUES USED
Single, double, half-double, and treble crochet, and working in rounds

For single crochet: see page 14

For double crochet: see page 16

For half-double crochet: see page 18

For treble crochet: see page 20

For working in rounds: see page 22

## METHOD
### Large flower
**Base ring:** Chain 6 and join length of chain into ring by working a slip stitch into 1st chain made

**Round 1:** Chain 5 [1dc, 2ch] 5 times into ring, slip stitch to 3rd of 5 chain at beginning of round. [6 spaces]

**Round 2:** [Chain 7, 1sc in 2nd chain between dc] 6 times, slip stitch to base of 1st loop. [6 spaces]

**Round 3:** Into each space work 1sc 1 half-double 2dc 4tr 5 double treble 4tr 2dc 1 half-double 1sc. Fasten off.

### Medium flower
**Base ring:** Chain 6 and join into a ring with a slip stitch into 1st chain.

**Round 1:** Work as Round 1 given for Large flower.

**Round 2:** Work as Round 2 given for Large flower.

**Round 3:** Into each space work 1sc 1 half-double 2dc 9tr 2dc 1 half-double 1sc. Fasten off.

## Small flower

**Base ring:** Chain 6 and join into ring by working a slip stitch into 1st chain made.

**Round 1:** Work as Round 1 given for Large flower.

**Round 2:** Work as Round 2 given for Large flower.

**Round 3:** Into each space work 1sc 1 half-double 8dc 1 half-double 1sc. Fasten off.

## Stamens

**Base ring:** Chain 4 and join length of chain into ring by working a slip stitch into 1st chain made.

**Round 1:** 13sc into ring, slip stitch to 1st sc at beginning of round.

**Round 2:** Working into front strand only of each sc of round 1, work 1sc, * chain 5, 1sc in 2nd chain from hook, 1hdc in each of next 2 chain, 1sc in next chain, 1sc in next sc of round 1 (1 stamen made), repeat from * 12 times omitting sc on last repeat. [13 stamens]

**Round 3:** Working into back strand only of each sc of Round 1, work 1 slip stitch, * chain 6, 5sc, 1 slip stitch in next sc of Round 1, repeat from * 12 times omitting slip stitch on last repeat. [13 stamens]
Fasten off.

## TO FINISH

Layer two different-sized flowers—large and medium, or medium and small—one on top of the other. Slip stitch together with cotton thread. Place stamens in center and secure with small, neat hand stitches.

Cut out basic leaf shapes from the scraps of fabric. Arrange leaves underneath flowers and sew into position.

Cut out a small circle of felt. Stick or sew to back of flower. Attach safety pin.

# Free-form Camisole

This pretty camisole is worked in free-form crochet. It is semifitted, with an asymmetrical hemline, contrast shell-stitch bodice, and fashionable double straps. Free-form crochet is worked in a very different way, since you create the fabric with your own pattern. This lingerie-inspired top is based on a favorite undergarment, which was simply traced onto a piece of paper to create a pattern. An asymmetrical hemline was added for an intriguing edging. Alternatively, you could use a commercial paper pattern and crochet to fit that. The basic instructions given here are for one size; use it as a guide to create a uniquely personal accessory that can be worn casually with jeans or more formally with a skirt or over a dress.

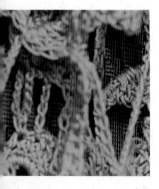  

# Making the Free-form Camisole

**SIZE**
Adaptable to fit any size

**MATERIALS**
Approx. 10 oz. (250g) Yeomans Cotton
Cannele or similar sport-weight mercerized
cotton yarn (see page 170)
Hook size D/3
Approx. 1 yd. (1m) ribbon, ⅛ in. (5mm) wide

**TECHNIQUES USED**
Single, double, and half-double crochet and
working in rounds

For single crochet: see page 14

For double crochet: see page 16

For half-double crochet: see page 18

For working in rounds: see page 22

For free-form crochet: see page 24

**GAUGE**
This camisole has a gauge of 20 chains to
3¼ in. (8cm), but working to an exact
gauge is not essential (see Tip).

**TIP**
**Gauge:** Don't worry about gauge too
much! If your motifs ends up a bit bigger or
smaller than the size given here, just add
more motifs to achieve the required size.

**METHOD**
Sketch out a basic camisole shape for your
body or trace around a favorite garment to
actual size onto squared graph paper to
make an accurate pattern.

**Bodice stitch**
Work in multiples of 5 with 6 turning chain.
**Foundation row:** Work [4dc, chain 2, 1dc]
in 7th chain from hook, * skip 4 chain [4dc,
chain 2, 1dc] in next chain, repeat from *
to end of row ending with 2 skipped
chains, 1dc in last chain, 3 turning chain.
**Row 1:** * [4dc, chain 2, 1dc] in 2 chain
space, repeat from * to end of row ending
with 1dc in turning chain, 3 turning chain.
Repeat Row 1.
Shape the bodice as required, referring
to your paper pattern.
On the lower edge of the front bodice,
make a chain to decrease the edge to
measure 16 in. (40cm) when finished.
Pin each piece of the bodice onto the paper
pattern in turn.

**Front free-form crochet**

Crochet as many of the following motifs as required:

**Rosette A**

**Base ring:** Chain 7, join with slip stitch.
**Round 1:** Chain 1, 12sc into ring, join with slip stitch into 1st sc, chain 3.
**Round 2:** 1dc into next stitch [chain 3, 1dc in each of next 2 stitches] 5 times, chain 3, join with slip stitch to top of 3 chain.

> Fasten off, leaving a tail for sewing.

**Rosette B**

**Base ring:** Chain 6, join with slip stitch.
**Round 1:** Chain 1, 16sc into ring, slip stitch to 1st sc.
**Round 2:** Chain 6, skip 2 stitches [1dc in next stitch, chain 3, skip 1 stitch] 7 times, slip stitch to 3rd chain of 6 chain.
**Round 3:** Chain 1, [1sc, 1 half-double, 5dc, 1 half-double, 1sc in 3 chain space] 8 times, slip stitch to 1st sc.

**Rosette C**

**Base ring:** Chain 10, join with slip stitch.
**Round 1:** 24sc into ring, slip stitch into 1st sc.
**Round 2:** [Chain 6, skip 2sc, 1sc into next stitch] 8 times, slip stitch into 1st chain.
**Round 3:** [8sc into next 6 chain space] 8 times, slip stitch into 1st sc.

**Rosette D**

**Base ring:** Chain 10, join with slip stitch.
**Round 1:** 24 half-double into ring, slip stitch into 1st half-double.

**Rosette E**

**Base ring:** Chain 6, join with slip stitch.
**Row 1:** Chain 1, 18sc into ring, chain 6. Turn.
**Row 2:** Skip 2 stitches, [1dc in next stitch, chain 3, skip 1 stitch] 4 times. Turn.
**Row 3:** Chain 1 [1sc, 1 half-double, 5dc, 1 half-double, 1sc in 3 chain space] 4 times.

**TO MAKE UP**

Pin each motif onto the paper pattern as desired to create a pleasing arrangement. Draw chain lines onto the paper template between all the motifs as a guideline for linking them together.

> Crochet linking chains between motifs

following the drawn lines, leaving the motifs pinned to the paper pattern. Insert groups of doubles at the points where two or more chains cross.

### Straps

Make two lengths of chain to attach to the peaks of the bodice, from front to back. Weave in any yarn ends.

Repeat for the back body piece.

### TO FINISH

Sew body and bodice along the side seams. Attach the crochet straps together with silk ribbon straps.

Thread a length of narrow silk ribbon along the base of the bodice, if desired. Tie into a small, neat bow.

# Beaded Handbag

This little handbag is suitable to be used at any time of day or evening. It is small enough to look dressy, but practical enough to keep your keys, cell phone, and lipstick in it. Tiny glass beads are threaded onto mercerized cotton and crocheted in simple single crochet stitches. The finished effect is vintage, especially when using values of one color, such as old rose, gunmetal gray, or beige. Contrast this with bamboo or tortoiseshell handles and line the bag with a pretty paisley print or favorite fabric and finish off the bag with a rosette, using either the vintage flower pin (see pages 150–3) or the flowers from the contemporary pillows (see pages 96–9).

# Making the Beaded Handbag

### SIZE

Approx. 9 in. x 11 in. (23cm x 28cm) measured from center of side gusset to center of opposite side gusset and from gusset to end of turn over for handles.

### MATERIALS

8 oz. (200g) Yeomans Cotton Cannele or similar sport-weight mercerized cotton (see page 170)

Approx. 1200 ⅛ in. (3.0mm) glass beads in matching color to yarn

Hook size B/1 and D/3 or hook size required to achieve gauge

Fabric, such as chiffon, for lining bag

Bamboo D handles (or similar)

Large sewing needle and cotton thread to match yarn

### GAUGE

This handbag has a gauge of 24 stitches and 32 rows to 4 in. (10cm) measured over doubles using a D/3 hook, or hook size required to achieve gauge.

### TECHNIQUES USED

Single crochet and adding in beads (see below)

For single crochet: see page 14

### TIP

**Adding a bead in single crochet:** Insert the hook through the stitch of previous row in the usual way, yarn round hook, and draw loop through. Slide bead close to the work, yarn round hook, and draw through both loops at the same time pushing the bead firmly on top of the stitch in previous row.

### METHOD

Side (make 2)

Before starting the work, thread approx. half the beads onto the yarn.

**Foundation chain:** Using D/3 hook, chain 69.

**Row 1:** 1sc in 2nd chain from hook, 1sc in each chain to end, chain 1. Turn.

**Row 2:** 1sc in each sc to end, chain 1. Turn.

**Row 3:** As Row 2.

**Next row (wrong side):** 1sc in next 2sc, * add a bead with next sc and every alternate sc, 1sc, * repeat from * to last 3 stitches, 3sc, chain 1. Turn.

**Next row:** As Row 2.

Repeat last 2 rows until work measures 8¾ in. (22.5cm).

Change to B/1 hook and work 6 rows sc without adding any beads.

Fasten off, leaving a tail for sewing.

### Base

Foundation row: Using D/3 hook, chain 57.

Row 1: 1sc in 2nd chain from hook, 1sc in each chain to end, chain 1. Turn.

Work 15 rows in sc.

Fasten off, leaving a tail for sewing.

### Corsage

Thread 26 beads onto yarn.

Base ring: Using B/1 hook, chain 4 and join into a ring with a slip stitch.

Round 1: 13sc into ring, slip stitch to 1st sc at beginning of round.

Round 2: Using the front strand only of each sc, work petal as follows: 1sc, * chain 5, attach bead, 1sc in 2nd chain from hook, 1 hald double in next 2 chain, 1sc in next chain, 1sc in next sc on Round 1 (1 petal made), repeat from * 12 times. [13 petals]

Round 3: Using the back strand only of each sc of Round 1 only work petal as follows: 1 slip stitch, * chain 6, attach bead, 1sc in next 5ch, 1 slip stitch in next sc of Round 1, repeat from * 12 times. [13 petals]

Fasten off, leaving a tail for sewing.

### TO FINISH

Lay the work out flat, then steam, and press lightly.

Take fabric for lining and cut out to size of crochet work adding ¾-in. (2-cm) seam allowance all the way round.

Cut a strip of fabric approx. 18 in. (50cm) by 4 in. (10cm) for the corsage.

With wrong sides together, fold crochet work in half and oversew or graft together the side seams.

With right sides together, fold lining fabric in half and sew both side seams, insert lining into bag and baste at the bottom corners.

In turn, lay the D-shaped handles on each side and gather fabric through from right side to the inside, enclosing the top of the lining and the bar of a handle, and secure with small, neat hand stitches to hem.

Take the strip of fabric for the corsage and fold in half lengthwise. Gather up this strip into a fan—use a running stitch along the bottom edge to gather. Allow any frayed edges to show along the outer edge. Sew the fabric corsage into position on the bag. Place the crocheted corsage on top and attach to the bag.

# Crocheted Bracelets

An irresistible trio of bracelets to crochet for you and all your girlfriends. Since these bracelets can be made from odd remnants of yarn, and each one can be made in less than hour. Experiment with different-colored ribbons, yarns, beads, buttons, and charms to personalise each one. Crochet a selection of bracelets; they make pretty accessories for all your clothes and add that necessary touch of vintage charm.

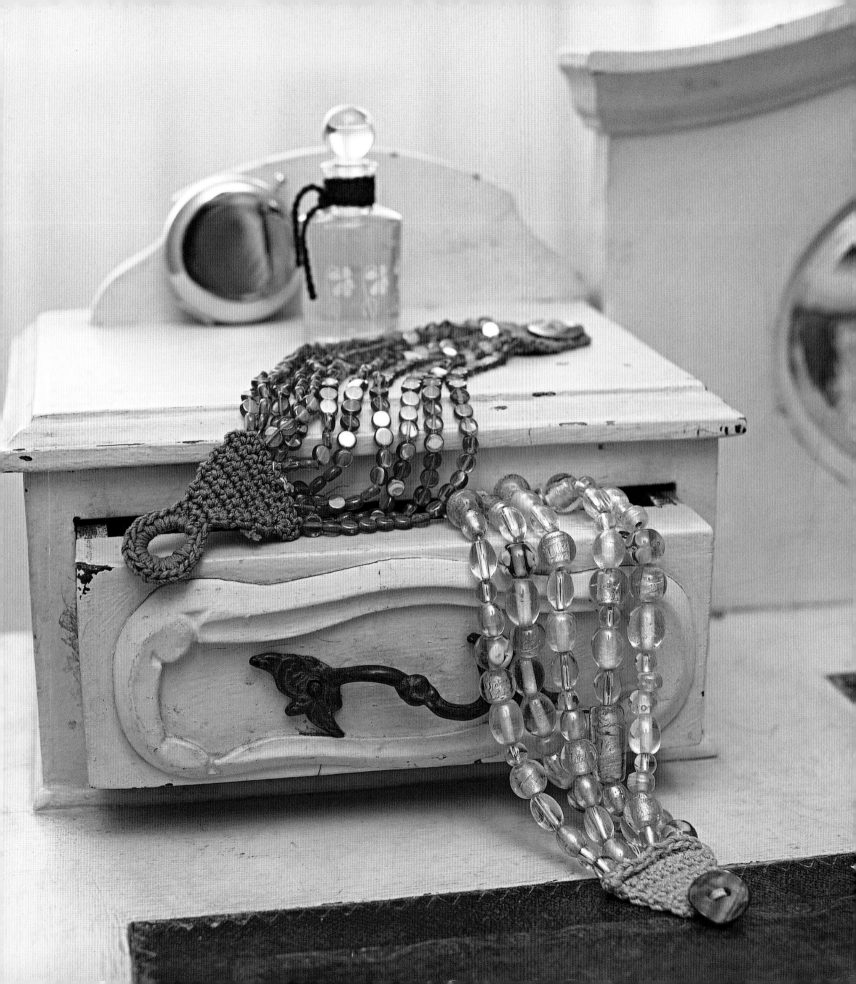

Ribbon charm bracelet

Beaded bracelet

# Making the Crocheted Bracelets

**BRACELET SIZE**
All approx. 8 in. (20cm) finished length

**GAUGE**
Don't worry about gauge too much!
Because these bracelets do not have to be
an exact size, you can add stitches until
they are the length required.

**TECHNIQUES USED**
Single crochet, cluster stitch, and crocheting
in charms (see pattern)

For single crochet: see page 14

**RIBBON CHARM BRACELET**

**MATERIALS**
Approx. 3 yds. (3m) satin ribbon, ¼ in.
(5.0mm) wide
Approx. ½ yd. (0.5m) satin ribbon, ¼ in.
(5.0mm) wide, in a contrasting color
Hook size E/4
10 charms, buttons, or beads of desired size
Polyester sewing thread in gold

**METHOD**
Before starting to work, thread the charms
onto the sewing thread in the order that
you want them attached. Work with the
ribbon and sewing thread together, adding
the charms as you crochet. Leaving a long
end for the bracelet tie, add a charm at any

point, and make a cluster as follows:
* Chain 4, yarn over, put hook through 3rd
chain from hook, yarn over, pull through
work, yarn over, pull through 2 loops on
hook, yarn over, put hook through same
space as before, yarn over, pull through
work, yarn over and pull through 2 loops
on hook, yarn over and pull through all 3
loops on hook (1 cluster made), repeat from
* 5 times to make 6 clusters.
  Fasten off, leaving a tail end.
  Cut the contrast ribbon in half. Double
one piece and knot this into the same place
as the long length of ribbon at the start of
the bracelet.
  Repeat with the second piece of the
contrast ribbon, starting at the other end of
the bracelet.

## BEADED BRACELET

### MATERIALS

Small amount of Yeoman's Cotton Canelle or similar sport-weight mercerized cotton yarn (see page 170)
Hook size H/8
Assorted beads or charms
Strong buttonhole thread and sewing needle
1 small button, ½ in. (1cm) in diameter

### METHOD

**Bracelet clasp (button end)**
**Foundation chain:** Chain 4.
**Row 1:** 1sc in 2nd chain from hook, 1sc in each chain to end. (3 stitches). [Turn each row with 1 chain.]

Increase 1 stitch at each end of next and every alternate row until there are 11 sc. Work 1 row sc. Fasten off.

**Bracelet clasp (buttonhole end)**
**Base ring:** Chain 10 and join into a ring with a slip stitch.

Work 20sc into ring and join with slip stitch.
**Next row:** Work 1sc into next 3 stitches, chain 1, turn. [Turn each row with 1 chain.] Increase 1 stitch at each end of next and every alternate row until there are 11sc. Work 1 row sc. Fasten off.

### TO FINISH

Weave in any yarn ends.

Secure one end of the thread to the fasten-off end of the bracelet clasp and thread the beads or charms to length required to fit around wrist—approx. 5½ in. (14cm)—and secure tightly to correspond to the fasten-off end of the other bracelet clasp. Thread approx. 5 rows in this manner.

Attach button to end without loop.

Motif bracelet

## MOTIF BRACELET

### MATERIALS

Small amount Yeoman's Cotton Cannele or similar sport-weight mercerized cotton yarn (see page 170)
Hook size C/2
6 buttons, assorted sizes
2 x 24 in. (60cm) length satin ribbon, ⅛ in. wide, in two contrasting colors

### METHOD

**Bobble stitch:** Work 5dc into next sc until 1 loop of each remains on hook, yarn over hook, and through all 6 loops on hook.
**Base ring:** Chain 6 and join into a ring with a slip stitch into 1st chain.
**Round 1:** Chain 1, 12sc into ring, slip stitch into 1st sc.
**Round 2:** Chain 3, 4dc into same stitch as last slip stitch until 1 loop of each dc remains on hook, yarn over hook, and pull through all 5 loops on hook [1 bobble made at beginning of round], * chain 5, skip 1dc, 1 bobble into next dc, repeat from * 4 times, chain 5, slip stitch into top of 1st bobble. [6 bobbles in total]

Fasten off leaving a long thread.

Make 4, 5, or as many motifs as required to fit wrist.

### TO FINISH

Weave in any yarn ends.

Attach the motifs together to make a band. Thread the two lengths of ribbon through each motif in succession and, at each end, finish with three buttons of various sizes, tying a knot between each button. Simply knot the ribbon to secure.

# Helpful Hints for Beginners

The section How to Crochet on pages 6–25 shows you how to work the basic stitches in crochet. The following information may be helpful to you when creating crochet projects either from this book or any other patterns you find.

You can choose to use the recommended yarns, or you can substitute others (see page 170 for information on yarn weights and types so you can choose suitable alternatives). Whether you choose to use the recommended yarns or ones of your own choice, you must check that you are working to the appropriate gauge, or the item you are making may turn out a very different size! Having said that, if you are making a throw, for example, and do not mind too much if it is a little bigger or smaller than the one shown in the pattern, then do not worry too much about stitch size. This is true of pillows, too, unless you wish to create a cover to fit a specific-size pillow form, when, of course, the gauge and the finished size will be important.

Certain yarns are easier to crochet with than others; those that are pliable and soft on the hands are the best for beginners, so select projects with soft cotton yarns to start. Crocheting with string (or twine) is not difficult, but because it is less pliable than cotton, it takes a little more dexterity initially, as indeed does leather, which benefits from being warmed before use.

## Pattern information

The instructions for crochet projects are usually given in writing. The basic abbreviations used in pattern writing are shown here, although these can vary, so always check the abbreviations guide in any crochet book first. One area of potential confusion is that U.K. terminology is different from U.S. terminology. In the U.K., single crochet is called double crochet, for example, while double crochet is known as treble crochet, and so on.

In some instances in crochet, it is easier to present the pattern information in charted form. This is particularly true of filet crochet, where the pattern forms a grid and can be most easily understood from a chart drawn on graph paper. Each "block" or "space" is represented by one square of the graph. Most patterns have elements that repeat. There is an asterisk at the beginning of the repeat element of the pattern, or it is placed inside two asterisks or brackets. The number of times this sequence is repeated is indicated outside the asterisks or brackets, along with any additional stitches required to complete a row.

## Practice makes perfect

You will find that the speed and ease with which you crochet is simply a matter of practice. It is a good idea to test your skills on very simple stitches, possibly making a few gauge swatches first. (You can always stitch them together later to make a patchwork pillow!)

## Abbreviations

To make the instructions for the crochet patterns easier to follow for beginners, very few abbreviations have been used in the book. However, the following lists cover the main abbreviations you may come across in other crochet patterns as well:

### abbreviations for crochet stitches

| | |
|---|---|
| ch | chain |
| dc | double crochet |
| dtr | double treble |
| hdc | half-double crochet |
| sc | single crochet |
| sl st | slip stitch |
| tr | treble |
| trtr | triple treble |

### other abbreviations

| | |
|---|---|
| alt | alternate |
| approx. | approximately |
| beg | begin(ning) |
| cm | centimeter(s) |
| cont | continu(e)(ing) |
| dec | decreas(e)(ing) |
| foll | follow(s)(ing) |
| g | gram(s) |
| in. | inch(es) |
| inc | increas(e)(ing) |
| m | meter(s) |
| mm | millimeter(s) |
| oz. | ounce(s) |
| pat(s) | pattern(s) |
| rem | remain(s)(ing) |
| rep | repeat(s)(ing) |
| RS | right side |
| st(s) | stitch(es) |
| tog | together |

# Caring for Crochet

| | |
|---|---|
| **WS** | wrong side |
| **yd.** | yard(s) |
| **yo** | yarn over (hook) |
| * | Repeat instructions after an asterisk or between asterisks as many times as instructed. |
| [ ] | Repeat instructions inside brackets as many times as instructed. |

## crochet hooks

Here is a conversion chart for the various systems of hook sizes—just in case you have old hooks you'd like to use but aren't sure what they are equivalent to.

## hook conversion chart

| Metric | U.S. | old U.K. |
|---|---|---|
| .60mm | 14 steel | |
| .75mm | 12 steel | |
| 1.00mm | 11 steel | |
| 1.50mm | 8 steel | |
| 1.75mm | 6 steel | |
| 2.00mm | B/1 | 14 |
| 2.50mm | C/2 | 12 |
| 3.00mm | D/3 | 10 |
| 3.50mm | E/4 | 9 |
| 4.00mm | F/5 | 8 |
| 4.50mm | G/6 | 7 |
| 5.00mm | H/8 | 6 |
| 5.50mm | I/9 | 5 |
| 6.00mm | J/10 | 4 |
| 6.50mm | | 3 |
| 7.00mm | K/101/2 | 2 |
| 8.00mm | L/11 | |
| 9.00mm | N/13 | |
| 10.00mm | P/15 | |
| 16.00mm | Q | |

If you have taken the time and trouble to create your own crochet textiles, you will want to make sure that they remain in good condition. The great variety of yarns on the market has necessitated some kind of international labeling standards for their care, which is usually indicated on the ball band. While some yarns can be successfully dry cleaned (check the symbols on the ball bands), many more are better washed carefully by hand. A few can be machine washed at appropriate temperatures. Again, all this information should be on the ball band.

## General hand-washing guidelines

• If the article requires hand washing, then make sure that you use gentle soap flakes, which must be dissolved before emersing the piece. Do not use very hot water to wash any wool yarn. Hand-hot temperatures are best.

• Always rinse the article at least twice in tepid water.

• Don't wring it roughly by hand; it is best to give it a short spin in the machine or, with delicate yarns, to wrap it in a towel and squeeze out the moisture gently.

• Pull the article gently into shape and hang it over a towel to dry, preferably on a flat surface.

## General machine-washing guidelines

The temperature guidelines found on machines are as follows:
140°F/60°C hot: Hotter than the hand can bear; the temperature of most domestic hot water.
120°F/50°C hand hot: As hot as the hand can stand.
104°F/40°C warm: Just warm to the touch
86°F/30°C cool: Cool to the touch.

## Care of special yarns

• Mercerized cotton, soft cotton, and fine cotton are best washed by hand. Rinse well. Squeeze gently in a towel to remove surplus moisture and hang flat to dry.

• Heavy-weight cottons can be washed in a machine on a cool wash; check the yarn label. Short spin only. Dry flat.

• Lurex, mohair, and chenille are best dry cleaned in certain solvents. Check with your dry cleaner. Air well after cleaning.

• String, leather, sisal, hemp, and raffia cannot normally be dry-cleaned and are best sponged down with a damp cloth and left to dry naturally.

# Substituting Yarns

Although I have recommended a specific Rowan yarn for many of the projects in the book, you can substitute others. A description of each of the yarns used is given below.

If you decide to use an alternative yarn, any other make of yarn that is of the same weight and type should serve as well, but to avoid disappointing results, it is very important that you test the yarn first. Purchase a substitute yarn that is as close as possible to the original in thickness, weight, and texture so that it will be compatible with the crochet instructions. Buy only one ball to start with, so you can try out the effect. Calculate the number of balls you will need by yardage/meterage rather than by weight. The recommended knitting-needle size and knitting gauge on the ball bands are extra guides to the yarn thickness.

## Rowan Yarns

### Rowan Kidsilk Haze
A light-weight blend yarn
Recommended knitting-needle size:
U.S. sizes 3–8; 3.25–5mm
Gauge: 18–25 stitches x 23–24 rows per 4 in./10cm over knitted stockinette stitch
Ball size: 230 yd./210m per 1 oz./25g ball
Yarn specification: 70% super-kid mohair, 30% silk

### Rowan Cotton Glacé
A medium-weight (between the double-knitting and 4-ply) mercerized cotton yarn
Recommended knitting-needle size:
U.S. sizes 3–5/3–3.25mm
Gauge: 23 stitches x 32 rows per 4 in./10cm over knitted stockinette stitch
Ball size: 125 yd./115m per 1¾ oz./50g ball
Yarn specification: 100% cotton

### Rowan Wool Cotton
A double-knitting-weight blend yarn
Recommended knitting-needle size:
U.S. sizes 5–6; 3.75–4mm
Gauge: 22–24 stitches x 30–32 rows per 4 in./10cm over knitted stockinette stitch
Ball size: 124 yd./113m per 1¾ oz./50g ball
Yarn specification: 50% merino wool, 50% cotton

### Rowan Big Wool
A bulky-weight wool yarn
Recommended knitting-needle size:
U.S. size 19; 15mm
Gauge: 7.5 stitches x 10 rows per 4 in./10cm over knitted stockinette stitch
Ball size: 88 yd./80m per 3¾ oz./100g ball
Yarn specification: 100% merino wool

### Rowan Summer Tweed
An Aran-weight blend yarn
Recommended knitting-needle size:
U.S. size 8; 5mm
Gauge: 16 stitches x 23 rows per 4 in./10cm over knitted stockinette stitch
Ball size: 118 yd./108m per 1¾ oz./50g ball
Yarn specification: 70% silk, 30% cotton

### Rowan Yorkshire Tweed Aran
An Aran-weight wool yarn
Recommended knitting-needle size:
U.S. sizes 8–9; 5–5.5mm
Gauge: 16 stitches x 23 rows per 4 in./10cm over knitted stockinette stitch
Ball size: 175 yd./160m per 3¾ oz./100g ball
Yarn specification: 100% wool

### Rowan Chunky Cotton Chenille
A bulky-weight cotton chenille yarn
Recommended knitting-needle size:
U.S. sizes 6–8; 4–5mm
Gauge: 14–16 stitches x 23–24 rows per 4 in./10cm over knitted stockinette stitch
Ball size: 153 yd./140m per 3¾ oz./100g ball
Yarn specification: 100% cotton

### Rowan Polar
An bulky-weight blend yarn
Recommended knitting-needle size:
U.S. size 11; 8mm
Gauge: 12 stitches x 16 rows per 4 in./10cm over knitted stockinette stitch
Ball size: 109 yd./100m per 3¾ oz./100g ball
Yarn specification: 60% wool, 30% alpaca, 10% acrylic

### Rowan RYC Cashsoft Double Knitting
An double knitting-weight blend yarn
Recommended knitting-needle size:
U.S. size 6; 4mm
Gauge: 22 stitches x 30 rows per 4 in./10cm over knitted stockinette stitch
Ball size: 142 yd./130m per 1¾ oz./50g ball
Yarn specification: 57% fine merino wool, 33% microfiber, 10% cashmere

### Rowan Biggy Print

An Aran-weight wool yarn
Recommended knitting-needle size:
U.S. size 30, 20mm
Gauge: 5.5 stitches x 7 rows per 4 in./10cm
over knitted stockinette stitch
Ball size: 33 yd./30m per 3¾ oz./100g ball
Yarn specification: 100% wool

### Rowan R2 Paper Yarn

An Aran-weight nylon yarn
Recommended knitting-needle size:
U.S. size 11; 8mm
Gauge: 14 stitches x 17 rows per 4 in./
10cm over knitted stockinette stitch
Ball size: 148 yd./135m per 1¾ oz./50g ball
Yarn specification: 100% nylon

### Other Yarns

### Jaeger Extra-Fine Merino Double Knitting

An double-knitting-weight wool yarn
Recommended knitting-needle size:
U.S. sizes 3–6; 3.25–4mm
Gauge: 22 stitches x 30–32 rows per 4 in./
10cm over knitted stockinette stitch
Ball size: 137 yd./125m per 1¾ oz./50g ball
Yarn specification: 100% fine merino wool

### Blue Skies Chunky Alpaca

A bulky-weight wool yarn
Recommended knitting-needle size:
U.S. size 9; 7mm
Gauge: 16 stitches per 4 in./10cm over
knitted stockinette stitch
Ball size: 100 yd./95m per 3¾ oz./100g ball
Yarn specification: 50% merino, 50% alpaca

Fine cotton thread specially designed for crochet lace is widely available in craft stores. The cotton thread used for the Lacy Pillowcase Edgings (pages 62–5), Organic Table Runner (pages 104–107), Heart-shaped Pillow (pages 144–9), Flower Pin (pages 150–53), Free-form Camisole Top (pages 154–7), Beaded Handbag (pages 160–63), and Crocheted Bracelets (pages 164–7) was obtained from:
Yeoman Yarns Ltd., 36 Churchill Way, Fleckney, Leicester, LE8 8UD, U.K.
www.yeoman-yarns.co.uk

Leather thonging is available in craft stores or from leather merchants/saddlery shops. The 1/16 in.- (2.0mm-) thick round leather thonging used for the Leather Tote Bag (pages 44–47) was obtained from:
J.T. Batchelor Ltd., Leather Merchants, 9–10 Culford Mews, London N1 4DZ, U.K.
Tel: +44 (0)20 7254 2962.

String (or twine) comes in various thicknesses and is not always labeled with an exact amount, so you may need to experiment with a single ball to start with. The String Ottoman (pages 54–57) was made with natural-colored kitchen twine, which is available at hardware and stationery stores.

Metallic wire is available in a variety of thicknesses in craft stores of from wire merchants, such as:
Metalliferous, 34 West 64th Street, New York, NY 10036.
Tel: 212-944-0909

# Yarn Suppliers

To obtain Rowan and Jaeger yarns, look below to find a distributor or store in your area. For the most up-to-date list of stores selling Rowan yarns, visit their website, www.knitrowan.com

**Rowan Retailers/USA**

**DISTRIBUTOR:** Westminster Fibers,
4 Townsend West, Suite 8, Nashua, NH 03064.
Tel: (603) 886-5041/5043 e-mail: wfibers@aol.com

**ALABAMA**
HUNTSVILLE: Yarn Expressions,
7914 S Memorial Parkway, Huntsville, AL 35802.
Tel: (256) 881-0260 www.yarnexpressions.com

**ARIZONA**
TUCSON: Purls,
7862 North Oracle Rd., Tucson, AZ 85704.
Tel: (520) 797-8118

**ARKANSAS**
LITTLE ROCK: The Handworks Gallery,
2911 Kavanaugh Blvd., Little Rock, AR 72205.
Tel: (501) 664-6300 www.handworksgallery.com

**CALIFORNIA**
ANAHEIM HILLS: Velona Needlecraft,
5701-M Santa Ana Canyon Rd., Anaheim Hills, CA 92807.
Tel: (714) 974-1570 www.velona.com
CARMEL: Knitting by the Sea,
5th & Junipero, Carmel, CA 93921.
Tel: (800) 823-3189
BERKELEY: eKnitting.com,
Tel: (800) 392-6494 www.eKnitting.com
LA JOLLA: Knitting in La Jolla,
7863 Girard Ave., La Jolla, CA 92037.
Tel: (800) 956-5648
LONG BEACH: Alamitos Bay Yarn Co.,
174 Marina Dr., Long Beach, CA 90803.
Tel: (562) 799-8484 www.yarncompany.com
LAFAYETTE: Big Sky Studio,
961 C Moraga Rd., Lafayette, CA 94549.
Tel: (925) 284-1020 www.bigskystudio.com
LOS ALTOS: Uncommon Threads,
293 State St., Los Altos, CA 94022.
Tel: (650) 941-1815

MENDOCINO: Mendocino Yarn,
45066 Ukiah St., Mendocino, CA 95460.
Tel: (888) 530-1400 www.mendocinoyarnshop.com
OAKLAND: The Knitting Basket,
2054 Mountain Blvd., Oakland, CA 94611.
Tel: (800) 654-4887 www.theknittingbasket.com
REDONDO BEACH: L'Atelier,
17141–2 Catalina, Redondo Beach, CA 90277.
Tel: (310) 540-4440
ROCKLIN: Filati Yarns,
4810 Granite Dr., Suite A-7, Rocklin, CA 95677.
Tel: (800) 398-9043
SAN FRANCISCO: Greenwich Yarns,
2073 Greenwich St., San Francisco, CA 94123.
Tel: (415) 567-2535 www.greenwichyarn.citysearch.com
SANTA BARBARA: In Stitches,
5 E Figueroa, Santa Barbara, CA 93101.
Tel: (805) 962-9343 www.institchesyarns.com
SANTA MONICA: L'Atelier on Montana,
1202 Montana Ave., Santa Monica, CA 90403.
Tel: (310) 394-4665
Wild Fiber, 1453 E 14th St., Santa Monica, CA 90404.
Tel: (310) 458-2748
STUDIO CITY: La Knitterie Parisienne,
12642-44 Ventura Blvd., Studio City, CA 91604.
Tel: (818) 766-1515
THOUSAND OAKS: Eva's Needleworks,
1321 E Thousand Oaks Blvd., Thousand Oaks, CA 91360.
Tel: (803) 379-0722

**COLORADO**
COLORADO SPRINGS: Needleworks by Holly Berry,
2409 W Colorado Ave., CO 80904.
Tel: (719) 636-1002
DENVER: Strawberry Tree,
2200 S Monaco Parkway, Denver, CO 80222.
Tel: (303) 759-4244
LAKEWOOD: Showers of Flowers,
6900 W Colfax Ave., Lakewood, CO 80215.
Tel: (303) 233-2525 www.showersofflowers.com
LONGMONT: Over the Moon,
600 S Airport Rd., Bldg A, Ste D, Longmont, CO 80503.
Tel: (303) 485-6778 www.over-the-moon.com

**CONNECTICUT**
AVON: The Wool Connection,
34 E Main St., Avon, CT 06001.
Tel: (860) 678-1710 www.woolconnection.com

DEEP RIVER: Yarns Down Under,
37C Hillside Terrace, Deep River, CT 06417.
Tel: (860) 526-9986 www.yarnsdownunder.com
MYSTIC: Mystic River Yarns,
14 Holmes St., Mystic, CT 06355.
Tel: (860) 536-4305
SOUTHBURY: Selma's Yarn & Needleworks,
450 Heritage Rd., Southbury, CT 06488.
Tel: (203) 264-4838 www.selmasyarns.com
WESTPORT: Hook 'N' Needle,
1869 Post Rd., E Westport, CT 06880.
Tel: (203) 259-5119 www.hook-n-needle.com
WOODBRIDGE: The Yarn Barn,
24 Selden St., Woodbridge, CT 06525.
Tel: (203) 389-5117 www.theyarnbarn.com

**GEORGIA**
ATLANTA: Strings & Strands,
4632 Wieuca Rd., Atlanta, GA 30342.
Tel: (404) 252-9662

**ILLINOIS**
CLARENDON HILLS: Flying Colors Inc.,
15 Walker Ave., Clarendon Hills, IL 60514.
Tel: (630) 325-0888
CHICAGO: Weaving Workshop,
2218 N Lincoln Ave., Chicago, IL 60614.
Tel: (773) 929-5776
OAK PARK: Tangled Web Fibers,
177 S Oak Park Rd., Oak Park, IL 60302.
Tel: (708) 445-8335 www.tangledwebfibers.com
NORTHBROOK: Three Bags Full,
1856 Walters Ave., Northbrook, IL 60062.
Tel: (847) 291-9933
ST. CHARLES: The Fine Line Creative Arts Center,
6 N 158 Crane Rd., St. Charles, IL 60175.
Tel: (630) 584-9443
SPRINGFIELD: Nancy's Knitworks,
1650 W Wabash Ave., Springfield, IL 62704.
Tel: (217) 546-0600

**INDIANA**
FORT WAYNE: Cass St. Depot,
1044 Cass St., Fort Wayne, IN 46802.
Tel: (219) 420-2277 www.cassstreetdepot.com
INDIANAPOLIS: Mass Ave. Knit Shop,
521 E North St., Indianapolis, IN 46204.
Tel: (800) 675-8565

## KANSAS

**ANDOVER:** Whimsies, 307 N Andover Rd., Andover, KS 67002.
Tel: (316) 733-8881
**LAWRENCE:** The Yarn Barn,
930 Mass Ave., Lawrence, KS 66044.
Tel: (800) 468-0035

## KENTUCKY

**LOUISVILLE:** Handknitters Limited,
11726 Main St., Louisville, KY 40243.
Tel: (502) 254-9276  www.handknittersltd.com

## MAINE

**CAMDEN:** Stitchery Square,
11 Elm St., Camden, ME 04843.
Tel: (207) 236-9773  www.stitching.com/stitcherysquare
**FREEPORT:** Grace Robinson & Co.,
208 US Route 1, Suite 1, Freeport, ME 04032.
Tel: (207) 865-6110
**HANCOCK:** Shirley's Yarn & Crafts,
Route 1, Hancock, ME 04640.
Tel: (207) 667-7158

## MARYLAND

**ANNAPOLIS:** Yarn Garden,
2303 I Forest Dr., Annapolis, MD 21401.
Tel: (410) 224-2033
**BALTIMORE:** Woolworks,
6305 Falls Rd., Baltimore, MD 21209.
Tel: (410) 337-9030
**BETHESDA:** The Needlework Loft,
4706 Bethesda Ave., Bethesda, MD.
Tel: (301) 652-8688
Yarns International,
5110 Ridgefield Rd., Bethesda, MD 20816.
Tel: (301) 913-2980
**GLYNDON:** Woolstock,
4848 Butler Rd., Glyndon, MD 21071.
Tel: (410) 517-1020

## MASSACHUSETTS

**BROOKLINE VILLAGE:** A Good Yarn,
4 Station St., Brookline Village, MA 02447.
Tel: (617) 731-4900  www.agoodyarnonline.com
**CAMBRIDGE:** Woolcott & Co,
61 JFK St., Cambridge, MA 02138-4931.
Tel: (617) 547-2837

**DENNIS:** Ladybug Knitting Shop,
612 Route 6, Dennis, MA 02638.
Tel: (508) 385-2662  www.ladybugknitting.com
**DUXBURY:** The Wool Basket,
19 Depot St., Duxbury, MA 02332.
Tel: (781) 934-2700
**HARVARD:** The Fiber Loft,
9 Massachusetts Ave., Harvard, MA 01451.
Tel: (800) 874-9276
**LENOX:** Colorful Stitches,
48 Main St., Lenox, MA 01240.
Tel: (800) 413-6111  www.colorful-stitches.com
**LEXINGTON:** Wild & Woolly Studio,
7A Meriam St., Lexington, MA 02173.
Tel: (781) 861-7717
**MILTON:** Snow Goose,
10 Bassett St., Milton Market Place, Milton, MA 02186.
Tel: (617) 698-1190
**NORTHAMPTON:** Northampton Wools,
11 Pleasant St., Northampton, MA 01060.
Tel: (413) 586-4331
**WORCESTER:** Knit Latte,
1062 Pleasant St., Worcester, MA 01602.
Tel: (508) 754-6300

## MICHIGAN

**BIRMINGHAM:** Knitting Room,
251 Merrill, Birmingham, MI 48009.
Tel: (248) 540-3623  www.knittingroom.com
**GRAND HAVEN:** The Fiber House,
117 Washington St., Grand Haven, MI 49417.
Tel: (616) 844-2497  www.forknitters.com
**TRAVERSE CITY:** Lost Art Yarn Shoppe,
123 E Front St., Traverse City, MI 49684.
Tel: (231) 941-1263
**WYOMING:** Threadbender Yarn Shop,
2767 44th St. SW, Wyoming, MI 49509.
Tel: (888) 531-6642
**YPSILANTE:** Knit A Round Yarn Shop,
2888 Washtinaw Ave., Ypsilante, MI 48197.
Tel: (734) 528-5648

## MINNESOTA

**MINNEAPOLIS:** Linden Hills Yarn,
2720 W 43rd St., Minneapolis, MN 55410.
Tel: (612) 929-1255
Needleworks Unlimited,
3006 W 50th St., Minneapolis, MN 55410.
Tel: (612) 925-2454

**MINNETONKA:** Skeins,
11309 Highway 7, Minnetonka, MN 55305.
Tel: (952) 939-4166
**ST. PAUL:** The Yarnery KMK Crafts,
840 Grand Ave., St. Paul, MN 55105.
Tel: (651) 222-5793
**WHITE BEAR LAKE:** A Sheepy Yarn Shoppe,
2185 3rd St., White Bear Lake, MN 55110.
Tel: (800) 480-5462

## MONTANA

**STEVENSVILLE:** Wild West Wools,
3920 Suite B Highway 93N, Stevensville, MT 59870.
Tel: (406) 777-4114

## NEBRASKA

**OMAHA:** Personal Threads Boutique,
8025 W Dodge Rd., Omaha, NE 68114.
Tel: (402) 391-7733  www.personalthreads.com

## NEW HAMPSHIRE

**CONCORD:** Elegant Ewe,
71 S Main St., Concord, NH 03301.
Tel: (603) 226-0066
**EXETER:** Charlotte's Web,
Exeter Village Shops, 137 Epping Rd., Route 27, Exeter, NH 03833.
Tel: (888) 244-6460
**NASHUA:** Rowan USA,
4 Townsend West, Nashua, NH.
Tel: (603) 886-5041/5043

## NEW JERSEY

**CHATHAM:** Stitching Bee,
240A Main St., Chatham, NJ 07928.
Tel: (973) 635-6691  www.thestitchingbee.com
**HOBOKEN:** Hoboken Handknits,
671 Willow Ave., Hoboken, NJ 07030.
Tel: (201) 653-2545
**LAMBERTVILLE:** Simply Knit,
23 Church St., Lambertville, NJ 08530.
Tel: (609) 397-7101
**PRINCETON:** Glenmarle Woolworks,
301 North Harrison St., Princeton, NJ 08540.
Tel: (609) 921-3022

## NEW MEXICO

**ALBUQUERQUE:** Village Wools,
3801 San Mateo Ave. NE, Albuquerque, NM 87110.
Tel: (505) 883-2919
**SANTA FE:** Needle's Eye,
839 Paseo de Peralta, Santa Fe, NM 87501.
Tel: (505) 982-0706

## NEW YORK

**BEDFORD HILLS:** Lee's Yarn Center,
733 N Bedford Rd., Bedford Hills, NY 10507.
Tel: (914) 244-3400  www.leesyarn.com
**BUFFALO:** Elmwood Yarn Shop,
1639 Hertel Ave., Buffalo, NY 14216.
Tel: (716) 834-7580
**GARDEN CITY:** Garden City Stitches,
725 Franklin Ave., Garden City, NY 11530.
Tel: (516) 739-5648  www.gardencitystitches.com
**HUNTINGTON:** Knitting Corner,
718 New York Ave., Huntington, NY 11743.
Tel: (631) 421-2660
**ITHACA:** The Homespun Boutique,
314 E State St., Ithaca, NY 14850.
Tel: (607) 277-0954
**MIDDLETOWN:** Bonnie's Cozy Knits.
Tel: (845) 344-0229
**NEW YORK CITY:** Downtown Yarns,
45 Ave. A, New York, NY 10009.
Tel: (212) 995-5991
Lion & The Lamb,
1460 Lexington Ave., New York, NY 10128.
Tel: (212) 876-4303
Purl,
137 Sullivan St., New York, NY 10012.
Tel: (212) 420-8796  www.purlsoho.com
The Yarn Company,
2274 Broadway, New York, NY 10024.
Tel: (212) 787-7878
Yarn Connection,
218 Madison Ave., New York, NY 10016.
Tel: (212) 684-5099
Woolgathering,
318 E 84th St., New York, NY 10028.
Tel: (212) 734-4747
**SKANEATELES:** Elegant Needles,
7 Jordan St., Skaneateles, NY 13152.
Tel: (315) 685-9276

## NORTH CAROLINA

**GREENSBORO:** Yarn Etc.,
231 S Elm St., Greensboro, NC 27401.
Tel: (336) 370-1233

**RALEIGH:** Great Yarns,
1208 Ridge Rd., Raleigh NC 27607.
Tel: (919) 832-3599
**WILSON:** Knit Wit,
1-B Ward Blvd. N, Wilson, NC 27893.
Tel: (252) 291-8149

## NORTH DAKOTA

**FARGO:** Yarn Renaissance,
1226 S University Dr., Fargo, ND 58103.
Tel: (701) 280-1478

## OHIO

**AURORA:** Edie's Knit Shop,
214 Chillicothe Rd., Aurora, OH 44202.
Tel: (330) 562-7226
**CINCINNATI:** One More Stitch,
2030 Madison Rd., Cincinnati, OH 45208.
Tel: (513) 533-1170
Wizard Weavers,
2701 Observatory Rd., Cincinnati, OH 45208.
Tel: (513) 871-5750
**CLEVELAND:** Fine Points,
12620 Larchmere Blvd., Cleveland, OH 44120.
Tel: (216) 229-6644  www.finepoints.com
**COLUMBUS:** Wolfe Fiber Art,
1188 W 5th Ave., Columbus, OH 43212.
Tel: (614) 487-9980

## OREGON

**ASHLAND:** Web-sters,
11 N Main St., Ashland, OR 97520.
Tel: (800) 482-9801  www.yarnatwebsters.com
**COOS BAY:** My Yarn Shop,
264 B Broadway, Coos Bay, OR 97420.
Tel: (888) 664-9276  www.myyarnshop.com
**LAKE OSWEGO:** Molehill Farm,
16722 SW Boones Ferry Rd., Lake Oswego, OR 97035.
Tel: (503) 697-9554
**PORTLAND:** Northwest Wools,
3524 SW Troy St., Portland, OR 97219.
Tel: (503) 244-5024  www.northwestwools.com
Yarn Garden,
1413 SE Hawthorne Blvd., Portland, OR 97214.
Tel: (503) 239-7950  www.yarngarden.net

## PENNSYLVANIA

**KENNETT SQUARE:** Wool Gathering,
131 E State St., Kennett Square, PA 19348.
Tel: (610) 444-8236

**PHILADELPHIA:** Sophie's Yarn,
2017 Locust St., Philadelphia, PA 19103.
Tel: (215) 977-9276
Tangled Web,
7900 Germantown Ave., Philadelphia, PA.
Tel: (215) 242-1271
**SEWICKLEY:** Yarns Unlimited,
435 Beaver St., Sewickley, PA 15143.
Tel: (412) 741-8894

## RHODE ISLAND

**PROVIDENCE:** A Stitch Above Ltd.,
190 Wayland Ave., Providence, RI 02906.
Tel: (800) 949-5648  www.astitchaboveknitting.com
**TIVERTON:** Sakonnet Purls,
3988 Main Rd., Tiverton, RI 02878.
Tel: (888) 624-9902  www.sakonnetpurls.com

## SOUTH CAROLINA

**AIKEN:** Barbara Sue Brodie Needlepoint & Yarn,
148 Lauren St., Aiken, SC 29801.
Tel: (803) 644-0990

## TENNESSEE

**NASHVILLE:** Angel Hair Yarn Co.,
4121 Hillsboro Park, #205, Nashville, TN 37215.
Tel: (615) 269-8833  www.angelhairyarn.com

## TEXAS

**SAN ANTONIO:** The Yarn Barn of San Antonio,
4300 McCullough, San Antonio, TX 78212.
Tel: (210) 826-3679

## VERMONT

**WOODSTOCK:** The Whippletree,
7 Central St., Woodstock, VT 05091.
Tel: (802) 457-1325

## VIRGINIA

**CHARLOTTESVILLE:** It's A Stitch Inc.,
188 Zan Rd., Charlottesville, VA 22901.
Tel: (804) 973-0331
**FALLS CHURCH:** Aylin's Woolgatherer,
7245 Arlington Blvd. #318, Falls Church, VA 22042.
Tel: (703) 573-1900  www.aylins-wool.com
**RICHMOND:** Got Yarn,
2520 Professional Rd., Richmond, VA 23235.
Tel: (888) 242-4474  www.gotyarn.com
The Knitting Basket,
5812 Grove Ave., Richmond, VA 23226.
Tel: (804) 282-2909

## WASHINGTON

**BAINBRIDGE ISLAND:** Churchmouse Yarns and Teas,
118 Madrone Lane, Bainbridge Island, WA 98110.
Tel: (206) 780-2686
**BELLEVUE:** Skeins! Ltd.,
10635 NE 8th St., Suite 104, Bellevue, WA 98004.
Tel: (425) 452-1248  www.skeinslimited.com
**OLYMPIA:** Canvas Works,
317 N Capitol, Olympia, WA 98501.
Tel: (360) 352-4481
**POULSBP:** Wild & Wooly,
19020 Front St., Poulsbo, WA 98370.
Tel: (800) 743-2100  www.wildwooly.com
**SEATTLE:** The Weaving Works,
4717 Brooklyn Ave., NE, Seattle, WA 98105.
Tel: (888) 524-1221  www.weavingworks.com

## WISCONSIN

**APPLETON:** Jane's Knitting Hutch,
132 E Wisconsin Ave., Appleton, WI 54911.
Tel: (920) 954-9001
**DELEVAN:** Studio S Fiber Arts,
W8903 Country Highway A, Delevan, WI 53115.
Tel: (608) 883-2123
**ELM GROVE:** The Yarn House,
940 Elm Grove Rd., Elm Grove, WI 53122.
Tel: (262) 786-5660
**MADISON:** The Knitting Tree Inc.,
2614 Monroe St., Madison, WI 53711.
Tel: (608) 238-0121
**MILWAUKEE:** Ruhama's,
420 E Silver Spring Dr., Milwaukee, WI 53217.
Tel: (414) 332-2660

Rowan Retailers/Canada

**DISTRIBUTOR:** Diamond Yarn,
9697 St. Laurent, Montreal, Quebec.
Tel: (514) 388-6188

## ALBERTA

**CALGARY:** Birch Hill Yarns,
417–12445 Lake Fraser Dr. SE, Calgary.
Tel: (403) 271-4042
Gina Brown's,
17, 6624 Center Sr SE, Calgary.
Tel: (403) 255-2200
**EDMONTON:** Knit & Purl,
10412–124 St., Edmonton.
Tel: (403) 482-2150

Wool Revival,
6513–112 Ave., Edmonton.
Tel: (403) 471-2749
**ST. ALBERT:** Burwood House,
205 Carnegie Dr., St. Albert.
Tel: (403) 459-4828

## BRITISH COLUMBIA

**COQUITLAM:** Village Crafts,
1936 Como Lake Ave., Coquitlam.
Tel: (604) 931-6533
**DUNCAN:** The Loom,
Whippletree Junction, Box H, Duncan.
Tel: (250) 746-5250
**PORT ALBERNI:** Heartspun,
5242 Mary St., Port Alberni.
Tel: (250) 724-2285
**RICHMOND:** Wool & Wicker,
120–12051 2nd Ave., Richmond.
Tel: (604) 275-1239
**VICTORIA:** Beehave Wool Shop,
2207 Oak Bay Ave., Victoria.
Tel: (250) 598-2272
**WEST VANCOUVER:** The Knit & Stitch Shoppe,
2460a Marine Drive, West Vancouver.
Tel: (604) 922-1023

## MANITOBA

**WINNIPEG:** Ram Wools,
1266 Fife St., Winnipeg.
Tel: (204) 949-6868  www.gaspard.ca/ramwools.htm

## NOVA SCOTIA

**BAADECK:** Baadeck Yarns,
16 Chebucto St., Baadeck.
Tel: (902) 295-2993

## ONTARIO

**ANCASTER:** The Needle Emporium,
420 Wilson St. E, Ancaster.
Tel: (800) 667-9167
**AURORA:** Knit or Knot,
14800 Yonge St. (Aurora Shopping Center), Aurora.
Tel: (905) 713-1818
Needles & Knits,
15040 Yonge St., Aurora.
Tel: (905) 713-2066
**CARLETON:** Real Wool Shop,
142 Franktown Rd., Carleton.
Tel: (613) 257-2714

**LONDON:** Christina Tandberg,
Covent Garden Market, London.
Tel: (800) 668-7903
**MYRTLE STATION:** Ferguso's Knitting,
9585 Baldwin St. (Hwy 12), Ashburn.
**OAKVILLE:** The Wool Bin,
236 Lakeshore Rd. E, Oakville.
Tel: (905) 845-9512
**OTTAWA:** Wool Tyme,
#2 – 190 Colonnade Rd. S, Ottawa.
Tel: 1-(888) 241-7653  www.wool-tyme.com
Yarn Forward,
581 Bank St., Ottawa.
Tel: (877) yar-nfwd
Your Creation,
3767 Mapleshore Dr., Kemptville, Ottawa.
Tel: (613) 826-3261
**TORONTO:** Passionknit Ltd.,
3467 Yonge St., Toronto.
Tel: (416) 322-0688
Romni Wools Ltd.,
658 Queen St. West, Toronto.
Tel: (416) 703-0202
Village Yarns,
4895 Dundas St. West, Toronto.
Tel: (416) 232-2361
The Wool Mill,
2170 Danorth Ave., Toronto.
Tel: (416) 696-2670
The Yarn Boutique,
1719A Bloor West, Toronto.
Tel: (416) 760-9129
**STRATFORD:** D&S Craft Supplies,
165 Downie St., Stratford.
Tel: (519) 273-7962

## QUEBEC

**MONTREAL:** A la Tricoteuse,
779 Rachel Est, Montreal.
Tel: (514) 527-2451
**ST. LAMBERT:** Saute Mouton,
20 Webster, St. Lambert.
Tel: (514) 671-1155
**QUEBEC CITY:** La Dauphine,
1487 Chemin Ste-Foy.
Tel: (418) 527-3030

## SASKATCHEWAN

**SASKATOON:** Prairie Lily Knitting & Weaving Shop,
7–1730 Quebec Ave., Saskatoon.
Tel: (306) 665-2771

## Acknowledgments

My sincerest and most heartfelt thanks and appreciation to the hugely professional and extraordinarily creative collection of people who have put this book together. The truly empathetic team at Quadrille Publishing: my mentor, Jane O'Shea, for her unswerving belief and encouragement; my rock, editor Lisa Pendreigh, for her discernment, expertise, support, and innate patience. The exceptional Helen Lewis and Ros Holder for inherent style and sublime design. The wonderful Graham Atkins Hughes who certainly helps to make craft sexy via his exquisite and inspirational photography. And Raoul, of course. Sally Lee for her tireless enthusiasm and creativity, amazing spirit, and friendship—this really wouldn't have happened without you! Pauline Turner for her invaluable professionalism, the hugely creative Hilary Jagger—thank you for getting involved—and my unique Hannah Davis. Also to Margaret Callaghan, who has the best vintage textile emporium in the country at 30a Upper St. James Street, Brighton. Stephen Sheard of Coats Craft UK for always championing me, and Kate Buller and her amazing team at Rowan Yarns for their incalculable and constant support. Tony Brooks at Yeoman Yarns for his invaluable sponsorship. Finally, Dolores York and her team at Reader's Digest for their belief in this project.